THE AGE OF M

Also by J. H. Reyner

RADIOCOMMUNICATION
THE UNIVERSE OF RELATIONSHIPS
PSIONIC MEDICINE
THE DIARY OF A MODERN ALCHEMIST

J. H. REYNER
A.C.G.I., B.Sc., D.I.C., F.I.E.E.

The Age of Miracles

LONDON
NEVILLE SPEARMAN

FIRST PUBLISHED
IN GREAT BRITAIN IN 1975
BY NEVILLE SPEARMAN LIMITED
112 WHITFIELD STREET LONDON W1P 6DP

© J. H. REYNER 1975

ISBN 0 85435 322 4

SET IN 11 ON 13 POINT PILGRIM AND
PRINTED BY CLARKE, DOBLE & BRENDON LTD., PLYMOUTH
USING CAXTON PAPER SUPPLIED BY
FRANK GRUNFELD LTD., LONDON
BOUND BY G. & J. KITCAT LTD., LONDON

CONTENTS

1	THE WORLD OF MAGIC	9
2	THE ILLUSIONS OF THE SENSES	16
3	THE UNMANIFEST REALM	29
4	PARANORMAL SENSITIVITY	38
5	TELEPATHY AND CLAIRVOYANCE	45
6	THE DIRECTING INTELLIGENCES	62
7	THE SENSITIVITY OF PLANTS	71
8	BEFORE YOUR VERY EYES!	78
9	PLANETARY INFLUENCES	88
10	THE DIMENSIONS OF ETERNITY	101
11	DOWSING AND RADIESTHESIA	115
12	THE MAGIC OF THE BODY	125
13	THE ASSESSMENT OF QUALITY	137
14	ATMOSPHERE	145
15	THE PLASMA BODY	154
16	MIND OVER MATTER	159
17	THE INDIVIDUAL MIND	168
18	THE AQUARIAN AGE	175
	Appendix—The Chemical Octaves	187
	Bibliography	195
	Index	197

LIST OF ILLUSTRATIONS

Figure		Page
1	DIPLODOCUS IN TROUBLE	19
2	THE ELECTROMAGNETIC WAVES	21
3	THE AUDIO SPECTRUM	23
4	THE CAGE OF TIME	30
5	ILLUSTRATING ACTUALIZATION OF POSSIBILITIES	32
6	BRAIN RHYTHMS	47
7	SIMPLE ATOMIC STRUCTURE	80
8	THE SOLAR SYSTEM	95
9	SLICE OF ETERNITY	105
10	CUBE OF ETERNITY	106
11	INTERLEAVED STIMULI	113
12	FORMS OF DIVINING ROD	116
13	DOWSER'S PENDULUM	119
14	MIRROR-IMAGE STRUCTURE	142
15	PYRAMID DIMENSIONS	148
16	TRANSIT OF SUN THROUGH THE ZODIAC	177
17	SIMPLE ELECTRON ORBITS	191

TABLES

1	THE PLANETARY SYSTEM	94
2	ESTIMATED WORLD POPULATION	181
3	SIMPLIFIED PERIODIC TABLE	188

CHAPTER ONE

The World of Magic

From time immemorial there have been magicians in the world—men and women reputed to possess the ability to over-ride the ordinary workings of Nature. They were held in high esteem in their generation, and either revered or feared by the populace. In modern times the developments of material knowledge tend to discredit any such beliefs, which are indeed regarded as an exercise of superstitious credulity.

Yet with the increased facility of communication in the present era there is accumulating evidence of a wide variety of apparently supernatural experiences which are exercising the minds of both the scientific fraternity and the public in general. What lies behind these curious abnormalities? Are they genuine phenomena or are they merely the products of imagination, or even trickery.

It is well known that many magical effects can be produced by deliberately-contrived illusions of various kinds, ranging from simple sleight of hand to subtle misdirection of the attention. Indeed, the technique of the modern illusionist is so highly developed that, except in small children, his tricks no longer induce any sense of wonder. We know that we are being fooled, and are entertained by the deception. Hence it is not surprising that the average individual tends to regard apparently supernatural phenomena with the same tolerant disbelief. Even if there is no outright trickery, it is taken for granted that some simple rational explanation exists, or will ultimately be discovered.

To some extent this is true. Little more than fifty years ago a person who could hold his hand in a small box which uttered disembodied voices and music would have been regarded as a veritable magician. Yet today such devices are in common use. They make use of scientific laws which are now well understood, but were quite unknown not many generations ago; and it is interesting to note that these laws were predicted by Clerk Maxwell in the middle of the nineteenth century, many years before their physical existence was established.

We live, indeed, in an age of scientific marvels which we take complacently for granted. It occasions no surprise that by pushing a button we can flood a room with light, or can 'see' an event which is happening at the other side of the world—or even on the moon. Our sense of wonder is becoming atrophied, and we only seek ever-increasing gratification of our desire for comfort.

* * *

Are we justified in assuming that in due time all will be revealed? Science is not prepared to accept this without reservations. It has established that the behaviour of the physical world is governed by well-defined laws which are basically of an elegant simplicity. These give rise to intricate patterns of structure and performance which have aroused in all the great scientists a profound sense of wonder. They are in the main consistent, which permits them to be manipulated with precision. Yet there are many phenomena which do not conform to these established patterns, such as telepathy, dowsing, spiritual healing and similar activities, for which conventional knowledge does not provide an adequate understanding, and which are therefore regarded as 'supernatural'.

This is no more than a complacent refuge. It implies that the world of conventional usage is beyond challenge, and that anything which does not conform to this pattern is abnormal. This is the exact reverse of the truth. The laws of physics and the associated sciences have been developed from experimental observations, which are themselves interpretations of the evidence of the physical senses, and it is the co-ordination of these sensory impressions which provides the highly-developed processes of logical reasoning. Yet it is known that the information supplied by the senses is of a specifically (and deliberately) restricted character, so that the intelligence which they convey is subject to certain inherent limitations.

For example, if our senses responded to a different range of vibrations the whole of the familiar world would entirely disappear, so that to regard it as the ultimate reality is a fundamental delusion. Supernatural phenomena must be interpreted as manifestations of a 'naturalness' of a higher order, to which the physical senses only respond to a limited extent. One can then postulate that communication with this superior world can be established through a range of *paranormal* senses which operate in addition to the conventional senses, but which in practice are very little used.

Actually the existence of these paranormal senses was well known to the ancient philosophers, who regarded them as part of the normal complement of human faculties, but their study and use became submerged in the flood of the apparently more practical developments of material progress. Nevertheless, there is ample evidence of the persistence of this faculty in the extra-sensory awareness possessed by many individuals. There is the curious rapport which exists between identical twins, or between people who are in a close emotional relationship. There are authentic examples of clairvoyance or 'second sight' displayed by certain people, usually of an essentially simple nature.

In most of us these faculties are only minimally developed, or even ignored, but they can be awakened, in which case they provide a greatly increased, and practical, understanding of the conditions of existence.

* * *

In the 1930's attempts were made by J. B. Rhine, of Duke University, N. Carolina, to discover a scientific basis for supernatural phenomena.[28] He suggested that if the effects were in fact produced by some form of extra-sensory perception (e.s.p.) it should be possible to reproduce it under laboratory conditions. He therefore embarked upon a painstaking series of experiments with a pack of special cards which were selected in random order, while an observer in a separate room was required to guess which card was being displayed. He used what is called a Zener pack, consisting of twenty five cards carrying five simple symbols, namely a square, circle, cross, star and a pattern of wavy lines. By the ordinary laws of chance one can expect five correct guesses out of the twenty five, but in fact he obtained significantly higher scores. Some particularly sensitive observers obtained more than twenty correct guesses. Various more sophisticated tests were devised, notably by Soal and Bateman in London,[32] which fully confirmed the validity of extra-sensory perception.

The value of this work lay in the establishment of parapsychology as a respectable science, but it is evident that the paranormal faculty is of much wider potentiality than mere card-guessing, as has been amply demonstrated by subsequent developments. The understanding of the possibilities has, however, been severely hampered by a too logical approach. Science has for so long been steeped in materialism that it assumes that it can find explanations in similar terms, but this is a fallacy because paranormal phenomena are, by definition, subject to laws of a different order which can only be interpreted by a superior quality of understanding.

One of the characteristics of the Universe is that it is essentially a structure of response to request. This is evidently true at the phenomenal level, for the whole behaviour of the physical world is conditioned by the interplay of responses to stimuli of various kinds. This has been established by scientific experiment, which is basically a process of assessing the answers to intelligently-formulated questions. If no answer is obtained, or if the result is not what has been expected, it is because the question has been wrongly or inadequately framed.

However, the nature of the answers will depend on the *quality* of the questions. If these are formulated in terms of limited logic of the senses, the answers will be in similar terms, and can only convey a limited understanding. If one is prepared to postulate the existence of a structure of a higher order, beyond the evidence of the senses, it is possible to ask questions of a different character and obtain answers of greater significance.

* * *

The existence of higher orders of intelligence and consciousness is a fundamental tenet of all esoteric and religious philosophies, and the idea that man's intelligence is the highest in the Universe is really ludicrously arrogant. Apart from the fact that it destroys the sense of wonder, which Einstein said was the fairest thing we possess, it entirely circumscribes the imagination. Perhaps the most significant development of the present century has been the growing acknowledgement by leading physicists of the occult nature of the concepts with which they operate. This aspect is very lucidly presented by Arthur Koestler in his book *The Roots of Coincidence* in which he discusses what he calls 'the various attempts to achieve a synthesis between the exact science of physics and man's intuitive intimations of deeper levels of reality'.[12]

There is a vast difference between the sense of wonder and mere credulity, which is a blind acceptance of convenient belief. The more one studies the mysterious Universe, the greater the evidence of intelligent design, and although many phenomena appear entirely accidental, they are in fact the fulfillment of a pattern existing within a superior realm not evident to the perception of the ordinary senses.

It is within this realm that we can find at least a partial understanding not only of so-called supernatural phenomena but also of many curious anomalies of ordinary existence. We do not have to degrade supernatural phenomena by attempting to bring them down to our level but can recognize them as *miracles*, in the true sense of the word. The usual definition of a miracle is a wonderful event or happening produced by a supernatural agency, but this is not really very helpful. It is tantamount to saying that a supernatural effect is produced by a supernatural agency! A more satisfactory formulation is that of the Russian philosopher Ouspensky who defined a miracle as the manifestation in this world of the laws of another world.[21]

This is a much more significant definition. By the implicit admission of the existence of higher orders of intelligence, it immediately provides a wider field of exploration. Moreover, since the experimental evidence confirms that the paranormal faculties are not subject to the limitations of the physical senses, one can postulate that they have been provided to permit communication with this superior realm, with results which are literally miraculous at the ordinary level.

* * *

Such concepts provide a new understanding of occult phenomena. In popular parlance the word has a certain mystical connotation, but it means, quite simply, beyond the (limited) range of conventional knowledge. Nor should it be interpreted as necessarily implying abstract speculation with which the ordinary individual need not be unduly concerned, for the ideas are of very practical significance. Quite simply, we normally live in a world of half-light, interpreted by a minimal use of our available faculties. The human mind is equipped with a remarkable range of additional senses which can communicate with the patterns of the real world and utilize them in a meaningful manner.

As was said earlier, these paranormal senses exist side-by-side with the conventional faculties, but whereas in the normal process of education we learn how to interpret the information supplied by the physical senses—which we thereafter take for granted—the paranormal senses are not so educated and hence usually only operate to a vestigial extent.

If these faculties can be awakened, we find ourselves in an altogether more exciting Universe.

It is with this possibility that we are concerned here. We must first try to envisage something of the nature of the extra-sensory realm. It is by definition a region subject to influences of a different order, to which the ordinary senses do not respond, so that it may be designated the *unmanifest world*. This does not mean that it is imaginary, for it has an entirely real existence, being responsible for the ordered direction of the whole of the familiar world, (in the course of which it creates a variety of everyday miracles which are normally completely unrecognized). We can then examine some of the phenomena which are literally supernatural at the ordinary level of experience but which may involve quite normal operations at a superior level of reality.

CHAPTER TWO

The Illusions of the Senses

Indian philosophy says that we live in a world of illusion (maya). This is surely not to be interpreted as implying that it does not exist since it evidently has for us a very tangible structure, which we interpret through the medium of the five physical senses. Nor in the ordinary way do we have any occasion to question these interpretations. We know, of course, that the senses can be deluded by a magician, while there are other interpretations which we know scientifically to be incorrect, such as that the sun travels across the heavens each day, whereas this is an illusion caused by the rotation of the earth. By and large, though, the senses provide an entirely adequate interpretation of the world in which we live.

Because of this we do not bother to enquire how this information is obtained. It rarely occurs to us to wonder how we are aware of the familiar objects and experiences, or even how we know that we are alive! In fact, this awareness is conveyed through a number of mechanisms of the most elegant precision, which we take entirely for granted, but which should be accorded a grateful recognition. If we can surmount our habitual complacency we find that we exist in a world of remarkable intelligence.

What do we mean by illusion? The word is derived from the Latin *ludere*, which means 'to play a game'; and this necessarily implies the existence of certain rules. Experimental evidence confirms that the Universe is essentially an ordered structure conforming to specific laws, and material progress is based on the understanding and application of those laws which govern the behaviour of the phenomenal world.

THE ILLUSIONS OF THE SENSES

The existence of apparently accidental, or supernatural, events and experiences must not be interpreted as arising from some breakdown in the structure, but as manifestations of laws of an unsuspected and possibly superior order which require a different quality of understanding. One is reminded of the tale of the traveller who stopped to ask the way to a certain place. 'Oh', said the local inhabitant, 'if I wanted to go there I would not start from here'.

Conventional knowledge based on the evidence of the physical senses is necessarily incomplete, since these senses are only concerned with the maintenance of an adequate relationship to the conditions of the phenomenal world—a situation which applies not only to mankind, but to the physical world in general, which is a beautifully and intelligently ordered structure.

We must indeed start from a new place, but this does not involve the rejection of ordinary knowledge. What is required is a better understanding of the limitations of the senses, and the reasons for this limitation. It then becomes possible to appreciate the remarkable intelligence of the human organism and the possibility of a greatly extended use of its potentialities.

*   *   *

The senses are basically mechanisms of response to stimulus. They translate the sensations of sight, hearing, smell, taste and touch into minute electrical signals which are transmitted through appropriate nerves to a co-ordinating centre located mainly in the brain. Actually many physical functions are governed by sub-centres, of which the most important is the solar plexus located in the abdomen, so that in medical parlance the controlling authority is called the Central Nervous System, but it will suffice to call it simply the brain.

Now these multitudinous impressions are, in themselves, meaningless. They have to be analysed by the brain with reference to an elaborate pattern of associations which has been acquired mainly by experience (though those concerned with the instinctive functions such as breathing, are innate). To take a simple example, if one touches a hot surface, the nerves from the finger tips will communicate a signal of appropriate intensity to the brain which will compare it with its existing standards of reference and, if it is deemed excessive, it will issue a command to the muscles of the arm to withdraw the hand smartly.

The reaction is very swift, but is not instantaneous. The transmission of the information along the nerves, both to and from the brain, takes a small but appreciable time, the speed of travel varying from about one metre per second in simple nerve fibres up to 120 metres per second in larger ones. In addition, some time necessarily elapses while the brain makes its calculations. The reaction to a hot surface would take something like one twentieth of a second (which might be too long to prevent serious damage to the tissues if the surface was red hot).

Larger animals are less fortunately placed. In a giraffe, for example, about one third of a second is required for an impulse from its foot to pass through its long legs and neck to its brain, and an even longer delay would occur (allowing for the calculation time) before a corrective command could reach the foot. It is believed, indeed, that one of the reasons why prehistoric monsters like the Diplodocus shown in Fig. 1 became extinct was that because of their size their reaction times were inordinately long, so that they were unable to bring their massive bodies to a halt in time to avoid disaster.

Where any appreciable calculation is required, the brain requires time to perform its operations. An emergency stop on a motor vehicle involves a delay of several tenths of a second before the recognition of the requirement is translated into action, and if the brain is tired or befuddled the delay may be even greater. On the other hand, if no physical action is required, such as in the internal assessments which create feelings, the reaction may be virtually instantaneous, though thoughts, which involve more complex assessment, take longer.

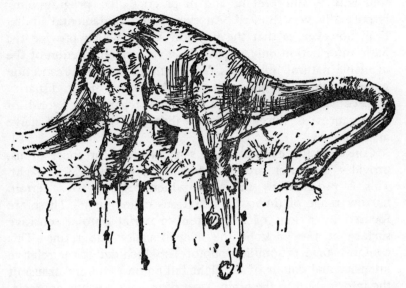

FIG. 1   Diplodocus in trouble

We need not pursue the mechanism in detail, though we shall refer later to some of the intricate operations which are involved in everyday activities. It is sufficient to note that the brain is, in fact, a highly-sophisticated computer capable of making the most elaborate calculations in a mere fraction of a second. It is these computations, which we take entirely for granted, which determine not only our behaviour, but the ability to reason on which all ordinary knowledge is based.

*   *   *

Now despite the enormous wealth of detail which the brain has to assess every second, the basic principles of its operation are simple. However, it is subject to two important limitations. One is concerned with the manner in which it translates the information with which it is supplied, and this it can only do in accordance with such directions as it has been given. No computer can assess information unless it is told how to interpret it, and in practice this 'programming' is normally very limited. An even more fundamental limitation, however, is that the physical senses which provide the basic information only respond to a very small fraction of the available natural influences. We shall see that this restriction is deliberate, but when we realize the extent of the disparity it becomes abundantly clear that to regard the world of appearances as the whole of reality is a ludicrously naïve assumption.

Consider, for example, the sense which, for most of us, provides the most prolific information—the sense of sight. This is provided by the eyes, which respond to a certain narrow range of (invisible) vibrations called 'light'. These are focused by a lens of transparent material onto a sensitive surface at the back of the eyeball called the retina. This contains some 130 million photocells which detect the relative intensity and colour of the light falling on them and transmit the information to the brain. Most of us have a vague appreciation of this mechanism. Yet actually the vibrations which produce the sensation of light are merely a small part of a wide range of intangible radiations called electromagnetic waves which permeate the whole of the physical world. Their properties depend upon their rate of vibration or *frequency*, which ranges from very slow rhythms, occurring a few times every second (and sometimes even slower) up to incredibly rapid variations of over one billion billion per second—in mathematical terms 10^{24}, which means one followed by 24 noughts!

These vibrations have been detected, and harnessed, by science, covering a vast range of phenomena. We can gauge the magnitude of the range from the diagram of Fig. 2 which indicates briefly the gamut of known radiations from brain waves to cosmic waves. Scientifically, the relative behaviour of different vibration rates is determined by their ratio rather than their numerical difference. Hence it is convenient, and more practically meaningful, to consider this enormous spectrum as a succession of stages, in each of which the range of

THE ILLUSIONS OF THE SENSES

	10^{24}	——
	100,000 ——	Cosmic Rays
	10,000 ——	
Trillions	1,000 ——	Gamma Rays
	100 ——	
	10 ——	X Rays
	10^{18} 1 ——	
	100,000 ——	Ultra-violet Rays
	10,000 ——	
Billions	1,000 —— =	Visible Light
	100 ——	Infra-red Rays
	10 ——	
	10^{12} 1 ——	Heat Waves
	100,000 ——	Microwaves
	10,000 ——	
Millions	1,000 ——	Radar
	100 ——	Short Radio Waves
	10 ——	
	10^{6} 1 ——	Medium Radio Waves
	100,000 ——	
	10,000 ——	Long Radio Waves
	1,000 ——	
	100 ——	
	10 ——	Brain Waves
	1 ——	

Vibrations per second

FIG. 2   The Gamut of Electromagnetic Waves

vibrations is ten times the frequency of the preceding stage; and in these terms the known radiations cover some 24 stages.

The greater proportion of these radiations are not detected by the ordinary senses. The eyes only respond to a small fraction of just one of these stages, covering a range of 400 to 750 billion vibrations per second, which is called visible light.

These particular radiations become entangled with the molecular structure of physical materials and are therefore reflected in whole or in part, thereby creating the appearances of the familiar environment. If only some of the radiations are transmitted, we experience the sensation of colour. Thus at the lower end we see the colour 'red', while increasing vibration rates create the successive colours of the rainbow, culminating at the upper end in violet. If all the radiations are transmitted equally, we obtain white.

Yet if the eyes responded to even a slightly different range of vibrations the whole appearance of the environment would change. Solid objects would disappear to be replaced by entirely new forms and structures. An X-ray machine, for example, can 'see' through the flesh of the body, and reveal its hidden structure.

There are similar limitations in the range of the other senses. Sounds are also produced by vibrations, though of a different type. They arise from a physical jostling of the molecules of the air which produces what are called sound waves. These are of much lower frequency, and are picked up by the ears which pass the appropriate information to the brain. (Sound waves can travel through other materials, sometimes even better than in air, but this need not be considered here). The human ear responds to vibrations of between roughly 30 and 16,000 per second, which is actually a fair proportion of the available 'sounds', but by no means the whole. Other animals have different ranges of hearing. Dogs can detect sounds above the limit of human audibility, a fact which is utilized in the 'silent' dog whistles often used. Bats

THE ILLUSIONS OF THE SENSES

find their way in the dark by emitting short bursts of supersonic waves of about 50,000 vibrations per second. These are reflected from obstacles in their path, enabling them to take avoiding action—a forerunner of the sophisticated radar systems of today (though these use electromagnetic waves).

Many man-made devices, such as depth-sounders or drills for brittle materials, use frequencies of several hundred thousand per second, while at the other end of the scale are very low frequency vibrations below the limit of audibility but which can cause intense discomfort and stress. Fig. 3 illustrates broadly the spectrum of sound waves as a succession of steps of progressively doubled vibration rate. In musical terms these are called octaves, in which any note has a similar sound to the corresponding note in the preceding

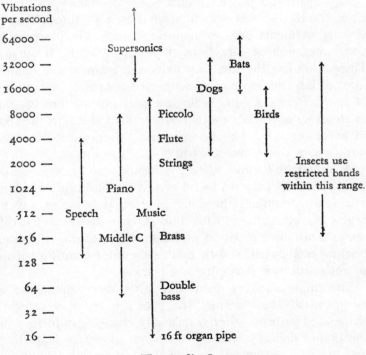

FIG. 3   The Audio Spectrum

octave, but is of higher pitch. It will be seen that there are many vibrations beyond the limits of human audibility.

* * *

The other senses are subject to similar, though less clearly defined limitations. Animals and insects possess a much more subtle perception of scents than is available to the human nose, and the same applies to taste and even touch. Enough has been said to indicate that the range of human sensory perception is peculiarly restricted; and there is a very practical reason for this limitation, which is connected with the second part of the mechanism, namely the interpretation of the information provided by the primary sense organs.

This again is a process which is usually taken for granted. Consider the sounds which assail our ears throughout our waking moments (and even during sleep). Every sound is a conglomeration of vibrations of many different frequencies. These stimulate the ears to provide the brain with a confused mass of information having neither co-ordination nor meaning of itself. How does the brain interpret one pattern of sound as the song of a bird, another as a human voice, or the sound of music, or the noise of a machine? More specifically, what bird, whose voice, and so forth?

A remarkable, and virtually instant, analysis is derived from reference patterns laid down in the brain by experience. The brain assembles the data in a tentative order which it begins to co-ordinate with information provided by other senses until by repetition and memory meaningful patterns become established, and thereafter the interpretation becomes so automatic that it is quite unconscious.

The impressions of sight are vastly more numerous and more initially bewildering. The eyes register a succession of shapes and patterns, often continually changing in form, which the brain gradually learns to interpret as people and objects, and even more remarkably translates the interplay of these shapes in terms of movement and distance. The process becomes so automatic that we give it no attention and fail to experience any sense of wonder. Yet there are recorded instances of people blind from birth whose sight is restored later in life. One would imagine that they would be overjoyed at this marvellous extension of their faculties. Actually they find the effort of learning how to interpret this vast influx of new impressions so exhausting that great patience is required to encourage them to continue! Add the impressions from the other senses and it will be clear that the brain has to acquire a very large network of associative patterns. Its burden is lightened by the fact that one of these patterns is that of meaning. A large proportion of the impressions recorded by the senses every second do not convey any significant meaning and hence are ignored.

On the other hand, there is a continual stream of internally-generated impressions based on fears, anxieties, emotions, and judgments of various kinds which are often imbued with quite spurious meaning, and if these are allowed undue preponderance the brain cannot cope, resulting in what is called a nervous breakdown.

Hence one can understand the reason for the restricted range of the physical senses. The various senses, in fact, convey just the right amount of information to maintain a satisfactory relationship to the conditions of life. Any more would not only be unnecessary, but could entirely overload the brain and cause the system to break down; and it may be noted that throughout the animal kingdom there is a certain correlation between the size of the brain and the range of sensory impressions available. The specific limitation of the senses, in fact, suggests the influence of intelligent design, for although it can be regarded as the result of supposedly accidental evolution, this is not incompatible with the possibility of intelligent direction by a superior level which will use natural processes for the implementation of its requirements.

* * *

The action of the brain as an interpretive mechanism has an implication of paramount importance, which is that it can only do what it is told. The study of its behaviour is known as *cybernetics*, from a Greek word meaning a steersman. This describes its operation very well, for its function is to direct the information which it receives through a succession of interrogating mechanisms which determine the ultimate response. This is the basis of the computers of which we hear so much today.

Now although the overall system is highly elaborate its mechanism is basically simple. At each stage of the process the electrical signals conveying the information are related to a previously-established pattern which determines their subsequent course. Hence the ultimate analysis (and the resulting action) is prescribed by the aggregate of these reference patterns, which is called the *programme*. The operation is described in more detail in Chapter 5, but it will be clear that it depends essentially on the provision of an appropriate programme.

There are two important aspects of the process. One is that the nature of the ultimate response is determined by the form of the programming. This means that the same information can produce differing responses. To take a very simple example, suppose the computer is given two numbers, say 3. If it is told to add them together it will give the answer 6, but if it is told to multiply them the answer will be 9; while if it is told to regard them as representing tens and units digits respectively, it will give the answer 33. It is clear that the interpretation of the vast amount of information which the brain receives every second depends entirely on the agreed programme.

Yet there is an even more significant consideration, which is that a computer cannot programme itself. Its instructions must be provided in the first place by an external (and superior) intelligence. Certainly a modern computer can be made to think for itself to a considerable extent, but only because it has been instructed how to do so; and, as is well known, it will often misinterpret its instructions with amusing —or sometimes not so funny—results.

In any case a computer is only a mechanism, and is still susceptible to human error. At one time my son made frequent use of a computer with which it was customary to add the code word 'buy' at the end of the information fed in, to denote that the data was complete and could be processed. One day he was using an alternative computer having slightly different programming. From force of habit he added the word 'buy' at the end of his data, to which the computer retorted 'What?'.

The human brain is in a similar situation. Despite its marvellous intricacy, it is no more than a mechanism which can only operate in response to programmes supplied by a superior intelligence. This is exercised by what we call the mind. This does not operate at the level of the ordinary senses, but is a function of the superior realm mentioned in the previous chapter. In the ordinary way, however, its direction is very perfunctory. Once appropriate programmes have been established by experience, these continue to be used without question, creating stereotyped habits of thought and action. If the mind can be aroused from its slumber it can supply a variety of fresh programmes which permit the brain to provide new and more intelligent interpretations.

We must not equate intelligence with logical reasoning. The intellectual function is, quite rightly, concerned with discrimination—the simple choice between yes and no. Yet there are many questions which cannot be answered in such simple terms, such as F. E. Smith's classic question to a stubborn witness—Have you stopped beating your wife? The true exercise of reason requires modified programmes which can recognize both yes and no as different aspects of reality. Moreover, such understanding will not be dependent solely on the evidence of the ordinary senses, but will include interpretations of the information derived from the much richer paranormal senses which are discussed later.

* * *

We set out to find how the senses provide us with information. We have discovered a mechanism of remarkable and elegant sophistication which appears to have much greater potentialities than are normally used. We know a great deal about how it works. Should we not also ask why? The brain, after all, is merely a highly-specialized component of an even more extraordinary mechanism called the body, which again we take for granted and with which we identify ourselves completely. Does this delicate and complicated structure exist for no other purpose than to meet the cosmic requirements of organic life?

This is altogether too narrow a view, for man has much more inspiring possibilities. He is equipped with faculties of a higher order, transcending the limitations of the body, which is merely a physical habitation. We shall be concerned to examine the clear evidence for the existence of these faculties and the development of a practical understanding of their application.

CHAPTER THREE

The Unmanifest Realm

Mathematicians delight in exploring the possibilities of imaginary domains in which the usual laws are replaced by different rules, and in many instances the actual existence of such domains is subsequently proved by experiment. We can make a similar excursion by postulating the existence of a superior realm beyond the evidence of the ordinary senses, and assessing the probable influence of such a realm on the experiences of the phenomenal world. We have seen that the perception of the physical senses is very limited, so that the appearance of the familiar environment can only be a partial portrayal of a much larger entity which is not detected by the senses. The German philosopher Immanuel Kant called this unmanifest region the *noumenal* world—the world of the mind—which he suggested lay behind and controlled the behaviour of the world of the senses.

Now the word 'phenomenal' is derived from a Greek root which means to show, so that the term is used to denote the world of appearances in general. But the Greek word has another meaning, when used in what is called its passive voice, which is *to come into being*. This is a much more significant interpretation, for it emphasizes that all the objects and situations of the sensory world are continually being brought into being by the passage of time.

We do not usually regard the events of life in these terms. We are, of course, familiar with the patterns of growth whereby, say, a tree will develop over the years from a seedling to its ultimate maturity. Yet we do not see events in general as 'coming into being', but rather as isolated experi-

THE AGE OF MIRACLES

ences in an inexorable progression from past to future; and because we appear to be inextricably involved in this mysterious transit we accept it as a natural and inescapable law. Actually the *sense* of time is one of the powerful illusions of the (ordinary) senses.

Plato likened the situation to that of a cave dweller with his back to the outside world, of which he was aware only as a result of a continually-changing pattern of shadows. Let us modify the analogy by imagining that he is enclosed in a circular cage containing only a narrow slit which slowly moves to reveal fresh portions of the world outside, as illustrated in Fig. 4. His awareness of the situation would be limited to a succession of fleeting glimpses of the landscape

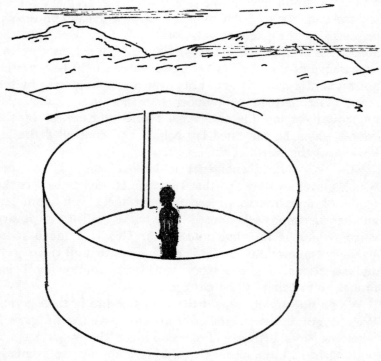

FIG. 4   The Cage of Time

which would follow one another in an apparently arbitrary manner. This is a fair analogy, for we have seen that our awareness of the environment is conveyed through a very restricted range of sensory impressions which follow one another in sequence. Hence events are literally brought into being by the moving slit of time, at a rate which we measure with appropriate clocks.

The significant feature of this analogy, however, is that the landscape so fleetingly revealed to the cave dweller is actually present all the time, so that what comes into being is a transitory succession of impressions of an already-existing reality. In similar fashion we can envisage that the familiar world of appearances is created moment by moment by the transit of time through an already existing real world.

* * *

Such would be Kant's noumenal world. It is evidently a realm subject to laws of a different order from those of the physical world, and for this very reason cannot be completely defined in material terms. A different quality of understanding is required, one which is more concerned with relationships. According to esoteric philosophy, the characteristics of this unmanifest region can be fully understood by higher levels of consciousness, the details being preserved in what are called the akashic records. By its very nature this information cannot be interpreted by the limited logic of the ordinary senses.

However, this does not mean that it is inaccessible. As said earlier, we are equipped with a range of paranormal senses which respond to influences of a superior order and which are concerned with the simultaneous awareness of the whole structure rather than its isolated parts. These faculties are normally undeveloped, but even in their vestigial state they permit the exercise of intelligently-directed imagination, which can provide a kind of intermediate understanding. In these terms the real world can be envisaged as a pattern of virtually infinite possibilities which are, for us, eternal, in

THE AGE OF MIRACLES

that they have a permanent and continuing existence. Within this pattern a variety of influences can operate which actualize certain of these possibilities in sequence and so bring into being a specific line of events. We can illustrate this by the simple diagram of Fig. 5, in which the irregular outline repre-

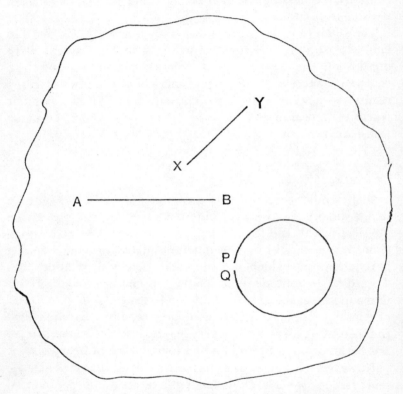

FIG. 5 Illustrating actualization of possibilities

sents a portion of the fabric of Eternity. Within this there is an infinite number of invisible points. If by conscious intention I draw a line from A to B, all the points in this line will have come into being by the successive actualization of the points in its track. But I have infinite possibilities in the process. I can start or stop anywhere within the area, maybe

THE UNMANIFEST REALM

in a different direction such as XY; or I can move the pencil point back on its tracks, as in the circle PQ. There is, in fact, the possibility of any number of shapes, in the course of which a whole range of different 'events' will be brought into being by the actualization of the appropriate possibilities.

This is a very simple illustration, which nevertheless includes the essential features. The surface of the paper contains within itself all the possible points, though they are mostly unmanifest. Even those that are actualized by the pencil still remain in existence. So that it is not difficult to envisage the real world as a similar pattern of possibilities, obviously of much greater potentiality, within which various influences travel to produce the manifestations at a lower level, some of which—though not all, as we shall see later—are detected by the physical senses. This idea was expressed by Plato in the Timaeus Myth, which discusses the pattern of the Creation. In the Timaeus he says:

'But since the pattern, which is eternal, could not be joined to any created thing, God made an image of Eternity progressing according to number—to wit, Time.'

The essential feature of this mechanism is that the transit of these influences in the real world creates manifestations in the phenomenal world which follow one another *in succession*.

* * *

The nature of time has been the subject of much discussion by learned individuals, which all too often is far from conclusive. One feels sympathy with Omar Khayam who, in Fitzgerald's translation,

> '... heard great argument
> About it and about; but evermore
> Came out by the same door as in I went'

There is no need here to become involved with such disquisitions because, in practice, we are not concerned with what time is, but how we are aware of it; and the answer to this is, quite simply, through the senses. So that we are conscious of the passage of time only through the interpretations of a time-sense, which like all the other sensory reactions is *acquired* by experience.

Actually this time-sense is two-fold, part cosmic and part individual. What can be called the natural time-sense is inherent in the organism. The performance of its many intricate functions involves an ordered sequence of cause and effect which is co-ordinated by the brain under the direction of an instinctive programme which is laid down at birth. This programme not only directs the natural rhythms of the body, such as breathing, waking and sleeping etc., but synchronizes them with a variety of cosmic rhythms, of which the most important is the rotation of the earth on its axis. (We shall see in Chapter 9 that this co-ordination is not confined to the human organism but operates througout organic life.)

All this results from the interpretation by the brain of appropriate sensory impressions, the instinctive behaviour being augmented very early in life by similar programmes derived from experience as part of the normal process of learning how to relate ourselves to the external environment. The significant point is that the physical senses are essentially mechanisms which respond to *changes* of conditions, which immediately introduces the element of time into the programmes, and the brain interprets its information in these terms. This means that we acquire, and accept, a mechanical awareness of the cosmic transit of time which creates the illusion of the succession of days and years.

However, concurrent with this we begin to create subjective programmes of a more individual character, less concerned with the hours and days of clock time, but related to the personal desires of the moment. This is clearly of a more variable character, its effect being so well known as to require little elaboration. A mother fraught with anxiety over the illness of her child will find time moving with leaden feet, whereas during the same interval of hours or days other people may be experiencing a succession of exciting events during which time gallops by all too rapidly. The individual time-sense, in fact, has a certain independence of clock time, being dependent on one's psychological state, which is determined by the level of individual consciousness operating at the time.

The distinction between clock time and individual time has an important bearing on the quality of one's experience which I have discussed in detail in an earler book.[26] In the present context it is sufficient to note that all phenomenal experiences are interpretations by a time-dependent awareness of successive manifestations created by the transit of an appropriate consciousness through the (existing) patterns of the real world.

* * *

This is a concept which will be understood more completely as we consider its practical implications in the later chapters. We must recognize that consciousness, which means, literally, knowing all together, is not an exclusively human attribute. We shall see (in Chapter 6) that the multitudinous activities of the phenomenal world are all directed by a series of non-physical minds, each subject to an appropriate consciousness. Hence we must envisage that the vast pattern of the unmanifest realm is enlivened by the simultaneous transits of these manifold consciousnesses. Animals (as well as man), plants, insects and even inorganic matter are continuously being made manifest by the transit of their relevant directing consciousness.

Each of these transits creates what mathematicians call a 'world line', so that every moment of clock time is intersected by a wide variety of different world lines, each playing its appointed role in the overall scheme. Hence no experience is really individual but is affected by all these intersecting influences, and it is these interconnections which determine the behaviour of the phenomenal world, in both natural and supernatural manifestations.

Now while these many transits are, in the main, subservient to cosmic requirements, human consciousness possesses additional potentialities in that it can operate at different levels. If we interpret consciousness as an ability to recognize relationships, it will be clear that the consciousness which directs the processes of logical reasoning, which is quite rightly concerned with the assessment of material phenomena, is necessarily of a lower order than that which is aware of the unmanifest causes in the real world. As a very simple illustration, a man who lives entirely in his own back-yard will have no understanding of the possibilities and relationships in the world as a whole—though he may perhaps become partially aware of them as a result of information from people who actually live there.

The human mind is equipped to respond to different levels of consciousness which have additional degrees of freedom within the eternal pattern and can move independently through the realm. Such higher levels are not subject to the conventional limitations of space and time—which do not exist in the real world—and can therefore establish connections with other parts of the fabric which we normally regard as the past or the future. Moreover, they can be aware of the conditions existing at the present moment to a greater extent than is conveyed by the ordinary sense-based interpretations.

This is no theoretical, or even abnormal, possibility because these wider excursions of the mind can be undertaken within the overall framework. We have, of necessity, to conform to the requirements of the cosmic transit which brings into being the successive manifestations of the phenomenal world—the hours and days of clock time and the course of history. The transit of individual consciousness has a certain degree of independence, so that it can not only vary in rate but can deviate from the path of clock time. The situation can be likened to that of a small child out for a walk with its mother. It can linger for a while to examine a flower which takes its fancy and can then run to catch up with the mother who has gone ahead.

THE UNMANIFEST REALM

Einstein spoke of time as a mollusc, which is a soft-bodied organism, though often enclosed in a rigid shell. A more flexible use of the individual time-sense will permit a certain movement within the restraint of cosmic time. Some experiences can be squeezed up and virtually discarded, while others can be expanded in both content and meaning. The employment of the innate higher levels of consciousness, in fact, can provide a greatly enriched understanding of the fascinating world in which we live.

CHAPTER FOUR

Paranormal Sensitivity

One of the oddities of ordinary experience is the occasional evidence of extra-sensory cognition, which can be defined as knowledge or awareness beyond the expectation of ordinary perception. This operates in many ways, ranging from simple rapport to the effects known as telepathy and 'second sight'. There are too many authentic instances of such phenomena for them to be entirely ignored, but all too often they are regarded as abnormalities, only experienced by people who are a little peculiar.

This is not so, for the effects actually arise from the exercise of an innate sensitivity to influences to which the ordinary senses do not respond. This is sometimes vaguely referred to as a 'sixth sense', of which the existence is now beginning to be accepted. It appears, in fact, that this is an entirely natural part of human faculty but is normally very indifferently used.

Such faculties will, by definition, be of an *extra* sensory character. We have seen that while the interpretations of the physical senses provide an appropriate relationship to the environment which is entirely adequate for the day-to-day requirements of life, the senses themselves only respond to a very limited range of impressions. Hence one can postulate the existence of a range of paranormal senses which operate in addition to the conventional senses, but respond to influences of a different order.

These influences, by definition, are not mere extensions of sensory impressions. They are concerned with the underlying structure of the unmanifest realm. Whereas the ordinary senses can only interpret successive glimpses of the pattern, like the cave-dweller in Plato's analogy, the paranormal senses see the pattern as a whole. They are instantly and simultaneously aware of the relationships which exist within the region, and recognize causes and possibilities which are not apparent to sensory intelligence.

It follows that the paranormal faculty must be of an extra-physical character. Conventional thinking assumes that the physical body is the whole of a man. Actually it is no more than a partial interpretation by the ordinary senses of an unmanifest entity in the real world. It is with this superior pattern that the paranormal senses communicate, so that they must be of a comparable quality. Hence any attempt to explain them—or any paranormal phenomena—in purely physical terms meets with little success.

There is, nevertheless, certain physical evidence of the faculty in the legendary 'third eye' which is considered to have existed in former times, but has become atrophied. There is in the front of the brain (in the centre of the forehead) a small lens-like vesicle called the pineal eye, covered by an almost transparent layer of skin. Its function is unknown, but it has been suggested that it may be a relic of an organ originally designed to receive paranormal impressions.

This is not inconsistent with the extra-physical character of the faculty, because the intelligence of a higher level can always utilize the laws of a lower level in the fulfillment of its requirements, and in fact does so in many instances.

The existence of the paranormal faculty is thus entirely comprehensible. Moreover, it is not confined to human beings but operates through a wide range of Nature. It must be understood, however, as operating at different levels of consciousness. Its simplest level is concerned with the production of a greater awareness of the existing situation, but its higher levels can contrive significant modifications which create supernatural effects.

* * *

There is in everyday life a rudimentary response to the paranormal senses which is responsible for what we call sensitivity. Why do we 'instinctively' like or dislike people whom we meet for the first time? You may say that this is a matter of type, or that it is a sub-conscious reaction to some physical attribute. It is more subtle than this, being really an intuitive recognition of harmony or antagonism between the individual essential patterns. We often have a similar intuition regarding situations, in some of which it feels right to act, while in others it appears better to refrain from acting. Indeed if we listen to these inner promptings we know very well that, in the words of Ecclesiastes, 'To everything there is a season, and a time to every purpose under the heaven'.

In addition, there is the sensitivity to the 'atmosphere' of places, which is discussed in Chapter 14, and which can be very marked. The pundits endeavour to explain these feelings by invoking the concept of the subconscious mind, but this is an unnecessary complication, for as we shall see later (in Chapter 6) the mind itself is a non-physical intelligence which directs the interpretations of the senses. More usually, perhaps, the feelings are dismissed as 'illogical' and hence of little or no practical significance. Yet the essential quality of these intuitive responses is that they are *not* logical, being interpretations beyond the limited logic of the ordinary senses. Intuition, indeed, is defined as 'immediate apprehension by the mind without reasoning'. This is characteristic of the paranormal senses, which provide an instant assessment of the relationships in the unmanifest realm without the necessity for the ponderous processes of thought.

It is the exercise of these paranormal facilities which permits the various forms of extra-sensory communication. Take, for example, the well-known rapport between identical twins who are intensely aware of each other, even if they have been separated at an early age, and have been known to suffer the same illnesses simultaneously. Here there is an inherently well-developed sensitivity which enables each to be aware of their essential patterns in the unmanifest realm.

We each have our underlying pattern. However, these are not isolated but are intricately interwoven in the fabric of the real world, which is not trammelled by the laws of physical space and time. Hence the paranormal senses, which have a similar freedom, are not limited to the interpretation of one's personal pattern but can respond to the influence of other patterns in any part of the fabric. This is no new idea, having been expressed by John Donne in the well-known quotation 'No man is an Island, entire of itself; every man is a piece of the Continent, a part of the main' (*Devotions XVII*).

One finds a similar idea in Jung's concept of a collective unconsious, in which all experience is shared.

* * *

Simple communities, not encumbered with the doubtful blessings of civilization, use the paranormal faculties as a matter of course. Laurens van der Post, in his book *The Lost World of the Kalahari*[34] gives an account of a vanishing race of African pygmies, whose scattered tribes are in extrasensory rapport; so that, among other things, an impending visit from a distant tribe is already known and prepared for before they arrive.

There is a recorded instance of an American Indian woman who was observed frequently to visit a tree with which she appeared to hold conversations. It transpired that she was actually talking to her daughter two hundred miles away who spoke to a similar tree in her own garden. In neither case, of course, did the trees actually speak, but they served as focal points for the establishment of a rapport between mother and daughter, so that they were able to communicate through the exercise of their paranormal faculties.

Even more remarkable are the activities of the natives of the Polynesian islands who practice the secret science of Huna. Their legends have been extensively investigated by Max

Freedom Long who found that their priests, or Kahunas, had developed the control of natural phenomena to an incredible extent. They are able to forecast the future with accuracy and even change the course of events if this is deemed desirable. Their bodies have a certain immunity to physical damage, and they can perform miracles of instant healing. They can, when necessary, control the local weather.

The validity of these legends was confirmed by Dr Brigham, the Curator of the Honolulu Museum, who had established friendly relations with the Kahunas, though without penetrating their secrets. This was ultimately achieved by Long after many years of patient endeavour, as recorded in his book *The Secret Science at Work*;[14] and a resumé of his findings, with particular reference to the medical aspects, is given by Dr Aubrey Westlake in *The Pattern of Health*.[40]

We need not discuss here the details of the Huna philosophy, which Long records at length. Its practical implementation is clearly a highly-developed exercise of the paranormal faculties which he ultimately discovered how to use himself. The essence of the Kahunas' belief is that all physical substances and situations are manifestations, through what they call 'aka threads', of an unmanifest casual entity with which it is possible to communicate by the use of higher degrees of consciousness.

This is a specific interpretation of the concept of an unmanifest realm containing the elemental patterns of all phenomena, which Jacob Boehme called 'the signature of all things'. It is a realm subject to laws of a superior order, but one can envisage that a higher level of consciousness can manipulate these patterns to create modifications of the normal manifestations.

* * *

Communication with this superior level is available through the latent paranormal faculties with which we are equipped, but which in most of us are *uneducated*. We are so accustomed to the automatic interpretations of the physical senses that we forget that these had to be learned during our early years. The myriad impressions to which the conventional senses respond are meaningless in themselves, but are gradually co-ordinated by experience to provide meaningful interpretations which we thereafter use unconsciously. The same applies to the paranormal senses, which we have to learn to recognize, and then to interpret by a similar education.

If properly developed, the paranormal faculty supplies programmes of a superior quality which enable the brain to provide expanded interpretations of conventional information, and at the same time creates an awareness of impressions of a different character which the ordinary senses do not detect. There are many manifestations in the phenomenal world which are beyond the range of the physical senses, but which are of equal importance in the structure, and it is to these influences that the paranormal senses respond.

The development of these extra senses, however, is not easy since they employ an unfamiliar language. Because of our customary complete reliance on sensory interpretations we expect the information provided by the paranormal senses to be in the same terms. Yet we are dealing with a different quality of information which cannot be interpreted in this way. It is derived from the recognition of the much more comprehensive patterns of the real world, which the limited logic of the conventional senses cannot comprehend.

There has to be a certain willingness to listen to these unfamiliar translations which are not expressed in words but involve an emotional understanding. This requires a conscious detachment which is initially very difficult, but which is absolutely essential. One can, in fact, understand that many simple folk who are not so engulfed in materiality exhibit a certain natural development of extra-sensory cognition.

The significant characteristic of the paranormal faculty is that it *enlarges* the quality of perception. It is an axiom in any structure of levels that a higher level of intelligence can comprehend and utilize the manifestations of a lower order.

Hence the operation of the paranormal intelligence will often make use of physical laws in the implementation of its requirements.

For example, it has been observed that when two people are in telepathic communication there are significant changes in their brain rhythms.[10, 20] Logical reasoning therefore seeks (without success) to explain the rapport in terms of some form of physical radiation. This is to confuse effect with cause, for the real rapport exists within the unmanifest realm, at a superior level which is not circumscribed by phenomenal laws, but which can use them for its purpose.

However, this is only one aspect of paraphysical communication. The human mind is just one of the intelligences in the Universe, and the paranormal senses can establish connections with many other behaviour patterns. We have already referred to the spectacular magical practices of the Kahunas, but there are many other practical examples of supernatural communication, one being the rapport which can be established with plants, as is discussed in Chapter 7. Another example is the practice of dowsing which is referred to in Chapter 11. Here there is communication through the paranormal senses with cosmic intelligences of various kinds, as a result of which involuntary physical responses are produced which provide answers to questions posed by the operator—responses which experience has proved to be entirely beyond mechanical contriving.

Finally there are the extraordinary phenomena of psychokinesis—the influence of mind over matter which is discussed in Chapter 15. All these effects can be understood as resulting from the operation of the paranormal faculty, which is really part of our natural heritage. If properly developed it can provide a much greater understanding, (and control) of the world in which we live.

CHAPTER FIVE

Telepathy and Clairvoyance

Let us consider some examples of extra-sensory phenomena. These are of two types, one involving the communication of information beyond the range of ordinary perception, which is loosely termed telepathy, and the other involving actual control of physical effects by supernormal agency. This is a very broad distinction since both types of activity can take many forms, but it will serve for the present purpose. We shall confine ourselves in this chapter to the former type, namely the awareness of events or situations beyond the conventional limitations of space and time.

Because of the authentic evidence for such phenomena there is today an accepted science of parapsychology which seeks to find rational explanations for the effects. In the process numerous attempts have been made to establish telepathic communication under rigidly controlled conditions. This is necessary since the highly-developed expertise of the modern illusionist demonstrates the ease with which the senses can be deluded, and the professional magician of today has a wide repertoire of effects—including apparently telepathic communication—which are acknowledged deceptions. Hence the scientific observer, while not necessarily pre-supposing deliberate trickery, is well aware of the fallibility of his senses and endeavours to eliminate any influences which might jeopardize his conclusions.

The early experiments with cards conducted by Dr Rhine and his associates have already been mentioned. Although they were necessarily academic in character they served to establish beyond question the existence of an extra-sensory faculty, and this has subsequently been demonstrated in more sophisticated ways, some of which have considerable practical application. This does not mean, however, that the behaviour is fully understood, for the real nature of the phenomena remains elusive.

Nevertheless the experiments are beginning to disclose something of the mechanisms involved. It is known, for example, the paranormal activity is accompanied by significant physiological changes. Neurological research during recent decades, with which one associates particularly the work of Dr W. Grey Walter,[37] has established that the complex operations of the brain involve intricate patterns of minute electrical impulses, in which there are certain predominant rhythms which vary with the degree and quality of attention. It has been found that in a number of instances there are significant changes in these rhythms during paranormal experience. In addition, it is observed that there are changes in blood pressure, muscular tension and respiration, while the oxygen supply to the brain is noticeably reduced. This is significant since it has long been known that mountaineers at high altitudes, who suffer from a similar lack of oxygen supply, experience 'light-headedness', and even awareness of themselves outside their body, which is evidently a paranormal state.

Now while these effects do not in any way divulge the causes of the phenomena, they do confirm that paranormal sensitivity is not abnormal, but is a latent exercise of natural faculties. This is particularly illustrated by the electrical activity of the brain, which can be examined by placing conducting pads at appropriate places on the scalp—a simple operation not requiring any surgery. These pads detect small differences of electrical potential which can be recorded by a pen on a slowly-moving strip of paper, producing a chart which is called an electro-encephalogram (abbreviated to e.e.g.) as illustrated in Fig. 6.

These small electrical impulses—about one millionth of the intensity of a torch battery—are constantly changing with the varying activity of the brain, but they are found to exhibit certain overall patterns which are significant. There are four such patterns, known as alpha, beta, delta and theta rhythms. Of these the alpha rhythm is the most important. It is a cylic variation occurring some 8 to 10 times a second

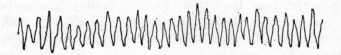

ALPHA RHYTHM

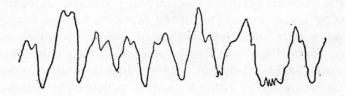

DELTA RHYTHM

FIG. 6 Brain rhythms

during periods of relaxed wakefulness, such as when the eyes are shut and one is thinking of nothing in particular. It disappears if the eyes are opened or if attention is given to some specific problem, when the brain appears to switch to a different level of activity, often acompanied by more rapid (beta) rhythms at between 13 and 22 cycles per second.

The alpha rhythm also disappears during sleep, being replaced by a larger but slower pattern called the delta rhythm at about 3 cycles per second. This appears to be a rhythm associated with the unconscious maintenance of the instinctive bodily functions, whereas the alpha rhythm is more concerned with conscious activity. It can, in fact, be regarded as bringing the brain to the threshold of alertness, which persists as long as the mind is relaxed. This tranquillity is disturbed if the eyes are opened, for then the brain is occupied with the interpretation of a vast influx of relatively insignificant impressions, or it may be required to undertake some kind of reasoning involving specific attention which may trigger a different level of activity.

However, a more conscious direction may disregard the flood of irrelevant impressions so that the alpha rhythm is not disturbed, and the brain remains potentially more alert. It is significant that during paranormal experiences the alpha rhythm is not only present, but its rate is often accelerated to 12 or 13 cycles per second—some 50 per cent above normal.

It is not practicable to discuss these brain rhythms in detail. Neurologists are aware of many variations and interactions, particularly in people whose mental processes are disturbed. During an epileptic fit, for example, the e.e.g. displays a number of random unco-ordinated spikes. Moreover it has been found that repetitive impressions which coincide with one of the basic rhythms can produce serious disturbance. A familiar example is the discomfort produced by a flickering light such as might be caused when driving along an avenue of trees on a sunny day. If the frequency of the flicker happens to coincide with the alpha rhythm it can cause a momentary blackout. Similar effects are produced by the subsonic vibrations which sometimes arise from machinery. These are below the threshold of hearing but can cause dizziness, loss of balance or recklessness, and it is believed that many unexplained accidents in factories or on motorways result from influences of this kind.

Finally there are the theta rhythms having frequencies in the range of 4 to 7 cycles per second. These appear to be connected with feelings of frustration, and if they are allowed to continue, possibly re-inforced from external sources, they can generate violent behaviour, and can even influence inanimate objects.

* * *

These various rhythms appear to be modified during conditions of paranormal activity, particularly during controlled experiments, which are often accompanied by considerable physical distress. One has to regard these findings with some reservation, since they may be induced, at least in part, by anxiety on the part of the subject. Simple telepathic communication would not appear to involve physical strain, the essential requirement being complete mental and physical relaxation, so that the brain is not pre-occupied with the interpretation of the bewildering and largely irrelevant impressions from the environment, and thus has the capacity to respond to programmes of a higher order. Some people dissociate themselves by going into a trance, but many exponents can exercise the faculty without outward signs of abnormality, though their alpha rhythm is usually found to be accelerated.

Where the faculty is being used to exercise control over natural phenomena, as with spiritual healing or the control of mind over matter (discussed in Chapter 16), there is a certain necessary depletion of vital energy which can produce physiological symptoms, but this is no more than the mechanism for the implementation of a pattern of a superior order.

One investigator has suggested, in respect of the cardguessing experiments, that the observed deviations from chance may be produced by some as yet unknown factor which obeys different laws. This is quite correct, but it is assumed that such laws will be of a physical character, which is not valid, and is like trying to lift a plank on which one is still standing. We must look for laws and influences of a different character, operating within a realm of superior intelligence.

* * *

The investigation of paranormal phenomena received a marked stimulus from a news report in 1960 which said that telepathic communication had been established between the atomic submarine *Nautilus* and trained observers on shore. This was officially denied, but Russian authorities claimed that they had been using such methods for years. In particular, they cited some experiments with rabbits, to which we will refer shortly.

In the ensuing years reports began to appear from various sources of the achievement of telepathic communication under controlled conditions. In particular, some experiments were reported in the Russian magazine *Sputnik* between a biophysicist, Yuri Kamensky, in Moscow and a friend Karl Nikolaiev, in Novosibirsk, some 1,800 miles away.[41] At a chosen time Kamensky was given a sealed package (selected at random from several similar packages) which on being opened was found to contain a metal spring consisting of seven tight spirals. This he examined attentively, fingering its convolutions. Nikolaiev wrote that he had the impression something metallic, gleaming, indented, looking like a coil. This is clear evidence of the transference of an idea quite beyond the bounds of coincidence, and there are records of many similar results in various parts of the world.

It should be noted that these experiments were all concerned with the communication of *ideas*, which appears to be instantaneous. Attempts to transmit language have not been so successful. In one series of tests the 'sender' listened to selected musical items of a type likely to interest his contact, but the recipient did not register any impressions of sound, though occasionally experiencing some associated visual response. Nor can messages be communicated in words, though clumsy attempts have been made to transmit them letter by letter using Morse code, which proved painfully slow.

All the evidence, in fact, confirms that telepathy, and extra-sensory cognition in general, operates at a non-physical level. We have seen that the ordinary senses are necessarily time-dependent, deriving their information from the reception of impressions in sequence. Moreover, if these impulses are to be transmitted by any physical wave motion there must necessarily be a time-lag in the process. The light from the Sun, for example, takes some eight minutes to travel the 93 million miles to Earth, while even from an object relatively close at hand like the Moon there is a time-lag of 1¼ seconds. Yet there appears to be no such lapse of time in telepathic communication, even with astronauts in space.

Extra-sensory perception is, by definition, not dependent on the physical mechanisms of the ordinary senses but operates within the realm of the unmanifest world which is not subject to the limitations of time or space. One can understand therefore that a higher level of consciousness will be aware of the pattern as a whole and will thus instantly recognize the connections and relationships which exist therein. To take a simple analogy, the pilot of an aircraft can be aware of the whole of the terrain beneath him, and will see not only its full possibilities but the probable development of events, such as an impending collision between two motor cars, before they actually happen.

* * *

Mention was made earlier of some Russian experiments with rabbits. These are of particular interest, because of their apparently impersonal character. In these experiments a number of newly-born rabbits were taken from their mother and housed in a submarine submerged beneath the ocean. The mother was kept in a laboratory ashore with electrodes implanted in her brain. At random duly-recorded intervals the young rabbits were killed one by one, and at the precise time of their death there was a sharp change in the brain rhythms of the mother.

As said earlier, this is no more than an indication that some telepathic rapport has been present. The significant feature of the experiment is that it shows that such rapport is not an exclusively human faculty but is of a cosmic character. Moreover, there is evidence of similar extra-sensory communication in other aspects of organic life, particularly in plants, as is discussed in Chapter 7; and although the existence of rapport is often detected by some physical response, it is clear that the mechanism is not of a purely physical character.

We have seen that all physical manifestations can be regarded as translations by the senses of already-existing patterns in the unmanifest realm. These senses are not exclusively human, for all organisms, and even inanimate matters, are equipped with appropriate senses. The many apparently independent manifestations of the natural world are all part of a greater whole, within which there exists the possibility of communication at a higher level than that of the physical senses.

This facility must not be regarded as the exclusive prorogative of man. All organic life is equipped with certain natural paranormal senses which, while possibly of a limited order, are fully developed. In man this is not so, for in his pre-occupation with materiality his paranormal senses have become atrophied. However, he is equipped with a mind having superior possibilities, so that if his paranormal faculties are properly developed, their potentiality is considerably greater. He can, in fact, establish a very practical communication with the underlying patterns in the real world, which is not confined to telepathy but can be displayed in a variety of other magical practices which will be discussed in later chapters.

* * *

It will be clear that the concept of the unmanifest realm has many practical implications, and it will be appropriate to examine some of these in more detail. It is important to recognize that the unmanifest world is not some kind of invisible super-space just beyond our grasp, but is a region in which the familiar laws of the phenomenal world do not operate. Now we have seen that the governing factor in the world of appearances is the illusion of time. Even the space which we take so much for granted is created by the interpretations of the physical senses, which are time-dependent. Hence the most important characteristic of the real world is that it is not subject to the limitations of time (and hence space) as we know it. Esoteric cosmology says that it has its own time, but this is on such an incommensurably greater scale as to be, for us, virtually infinite.[21, 26]

We must therefore envisage the real world not as a structure of objects and sequences, but as a field of already-existing possibilities which are interpreted in succession by the senses of the phenomenal world. This does not necessarily imply a grim pre-destination, for it is the possibilities which are eternal, and not the actualizations, which can be varied. This can be illustrated by a simple analogy. Suppose I take a walk through the countryside. I shall encounter continually changing situations on the way but, in general, this will cause no surprise because my reason tells me that they are already there. The village I have just left has entirely disappeared, but I do not question its continued existence. Similarly, my destination will come into being miraculously before my very eyes. I am, indeed, making a journey through an already-existing landscape, much of which I may barely notice if my attention is entirely pre-occupied with arriving at my destination.

This same journey, however, can be made in a variety of ways. I can explore alternative routes, particularly if I have time to spare, and in so doing I may encounter different situations. Even if I adhere to the original path I may notice some of the incidental items on the way which were previously ignored. All of which will be an additional actualization of some of the many possibilities which are there all the time.

Similarly one can envisage that various forms of consciousness make their appropriate journeys through the elaborate 'landscape' of possibilities, bringing into being those which lie in their path. The appearances of the physical world are created by the transit of an impersonal consciousness which is directed by cosmic intelligences; but there are simultaneous transits of individual consciousness (not exclusively human) which actualize additional possibilities within the pattern. These are responsible for the behaviour of the world of Nature which has certain degrees of freedom within the cosmic sequence.

Man has still greater potentialities, for he can respond to a number of separate levels of consciousness. The most mechanical level is entirely constrained by the impersonal requirements of the cosmic transit, but the higher levels are not so circumscribed. They can traverse other parts of the region, thereby creating entirely new experiences, often beyond the limitations of the cosmic transit. It is this facility which permits the variety of supernatural experiences.

* * *

An idea which is helpful in exploring paranormal possibilities is the concept of time-body which one finds in Swedenborg's dissertations on memory. This is another subject about which there is much loose thinking. It is often believed that every experience is stored in the recesses of the mind, as if in boxes which can be opened at will. This is a very superficial assumption which is far from the truth. Actually there are two distinct kinds of memory, neither of which is stored in the mind, which is a directing intelligence not concerned with detail.

Ordinary memory is a physical function (though perhaps this is not generally realized). It is of two types, physiological and psychological. Physiological memory is concerned with the instinctive behaviour of the body as an organized structure. The individual cells and organs respond to stimuli of various kinds, partly chemical, partly electrical, which are co-ordinated by an appropriate authority to maintain the maintenance of the bodily structure—an operation which, in the main, is performed with remarkable efficiency.

When we speak of memory, however, we are more usually concerned with the processes of learning and reminscence.

These are operations involving the brain, which receives information from the senses and translates it into appropriate action. The significant aspect of the process is that in some way the information, and the relevant response, can be stored for future use. This is entirely necessary for our survival, though how it comes about we do not bother to question. At one time it was thought that every experience was permanently recorded in the brain, but this would be neither economical nor practicable, for the system would soon become saturated and unable to accept any further information.

The actual mechanism is much more flexible (and more intelligent) and is worth discussing very briefly because of its ingenuity. In very simple terms, the brain is an assembly of interconnected specialized cells called neurones which have a certain discriminative ability. This means that they can compare the minute electrical signals which they receive with certain pre-established conditions of reference, as a result of which an appropriate signal is passed on to further neurones which will respond (or not) according to their own terms of reference. Any given item of information is thus routed through a succession of 'gates' until it arrives at an appropriate part of the network which dictates the action required. At this point a feedback signal is generated which clears all the previous links in the chain and leaves them ready to respond to further information. Hence the cells are not permanently engaged, which provides virtually unlimited flexibility.

The situation is similar to that in a modern telephone exchange. The dialling of a call sets in motion a complex system of mechanisms through which a connection is established with the wanted subscriber; but to maintain the whole network in operation throughout the conversation would preclude its use for any other calls and would require an inordinate multiplicity of equipment. Hence each mechanism simply passes on the relevant information and is then released for further use.

In similar fashion the information conveyed by the senses is passed along an appropriate associative track in the brain, and since there are some 10,000 million cells in the cerebral cortex there is clearly a vast range of possible routes. There is, however, an important additional feature in the system, which is that once any particular route has been used it is pre-disposed to react in the same way to any subsequent information of the same kind.

This is believed to result from small changes in the internal structure of the cells. Living cells contain in their nucleus a number of long thread-like molecules which are assemblies of relatively simple amino acids, the build-up of the individual links containing the genetic code. In a neurone cell a signal of sufficient intensity produces a small modification of this pattern which causes the cell to 'fire', i.e. to generate an appropriate response signal. After a short recovery period it reverts to normal, but there remains a tendency to respond more readily to any subsequent signal of a similar nature. This is strengthened by repetition, so that after a short time the reaction becomes stereotyped, resulting in the formation of a habit.

The system, in fact, begins to acquire a *memory*, which operates in a variety of ways. The very fact that you can read these words depends on the memory of a process learned many years ago which has become so well established that it requires no conscious attention; and the majority of behaviour is based on similar unconscious memory. At the same time, there is what may be called voluntary memory, which happens when some impression triggers a train of associations relating to some previous experience, so that the event is 'remembered'. It is not completely re-experienced because there is a significant factor missing in the pattern, namely the element of 'this is happening now', but the recollection can on occasions be very vivid.

Now, an essential part of the mechanism of memory is the element of *meaning*. There are numerous trivial impressions which have no particular significance. These do not reach the threshold level and are therefore ignored; but those which do have some relative importance will initiate an appropriate associative pattern, and this can be re-activated by subsequent impressions having the same quality of meaning.

The difficulty is that meaning in itself is a very complex pattern, and moreover is continually changing. What is important in one situation may be irrelevant in another, and in any case meaning is considerably influenced by one's internal state. As a result the brain makes all kinds of wrong connections, even to the extent of 'remembering' things that never happened, so that ordinary memory is not only elusive but can be very unreliable.

The whole process is evidently very complex. As a matter of interest it is believed that the whole network is continually being scanned like the elements in a television picture to determine the appropriate action, and it is this process which is responsible for the brain rhythms mentioned earlier. Yet this very complexity contains the possibility of providing entirely different interpretations of the continual influx of impressions by the direction of more conscious programmes.

* * *

However, there is a different kind of memory which is true. This arises from the pattern in the superior realm in which every experience *is* permanently recorded. Swedenborg called this the interior memory and suggested that this was the legendary book of life, which was opened at death. It can be understood in practical terms by the concept of time-body. We have seen that the events of life are created by the transit of consciousness through the realm of eternal possibilities, in the course of which there is an actualization of those possibilities which lie in its path. However, every possibility which is so actualized is slightly modified. It no longer possesses its pristine freedom, so that the transit of consciousness leaves a kind of trace in the overall pattern which is (relatively) permanent.

This is the time-body. It is created by the transit of the relevant consciousness, which in man is (or can be) individual.

Similarly, all the manifestations in the phenomenal world have their own time-body, generated by the transit of the appropriate consciousness, which in general is *not* individual but is of a cosmic nature. All these time-bodies are interwoven in the fabric of Eternity so that they interact. This means that the time-body of a man has numerous, usually unsuspected, connections with the time-bodies of all the people and situations encountered during his life. One can see again the truth of John Donne's saying that no man is an island, and begin to appreciate the poverty of purely sense-based perception.

* * *

It is evident that the concept of the fabric of Eternity opens up new horizons. It makes it possible to understand, entirely practically, the connections between people and situations quite beyond the limitations of the space and time of the senses. For example, in the experiment with the rabbits, the time-bodies of the mother and her offspring are closely intertwined so that the abrupt termination of the time-body of each of the infants creates a disturbance to which the mother responds through her natural paranormal awareness.

We must not be so stupidly exotistic as to imagine that the paranormal senses are exclusively human—any more than are the physical senses. All Nature is controlled by sense mechanisms of one form or another, but it also responds to a variety of extra-sensory influences, which are equally available to man. Telepathy, in fact, is a natural function, but it cannot be exercised if one's awareness is entirely absorbed in physical interpretations.

The same applies to clairvoyance, which is usually loosely regarded as the ability to see the future. This is only a part of the function, for clairvoyance—literally clear vision—involves an objective awareness of relationships in the patterns of the real world. The higher levels of individual consciousness are not trammelled by the transit of cosmic time, but can move through any part of the Eternal fabric. This not only permits an appreciation of the real relationships existing at the present moment, but is able to see the situations which will be encountered *if the present line of time is continued*, and to this extent foresee the future.

This may take the form of a premonition, or less commonly an actual vision during a state of trance or relaxation. There are too many authentic instances of this 'second sight' to warrant detailed citation, but there are certain interesting features which may be noted. One is that whereas telepathic rapport is most easily established where there is a strong personal or individual bond, the most significant clairvoyant experiences are of a more objective character, providing foreknowledge or assessments of situations with which the seer is not personally involved.

Now we have seen that the paranormal senses are emotional—i.e. they are concerned with relationships. These the brain can assess without words (if it has been suitably programmed), but it has difficulty in interpreting them in physical terms because of its unfamiliarity with the language, and this difficulty is aggravated if there is any personal involvement. Hence attempts to use clairvoyance for personal gain are rarely successful, for its indications will be distorted by the limited understanding of the ordinary senses.

This was amusingly illustrated in a novel by John Buchan entitled *The Gap in the Curtain*. In this a professor who had psychic powers arranged for four different people to become briefly clairvoyant. Each chose to see the future in respect of his own particular interest. In each case the prophetic vision came true, but in a quite unexpected and unprofitable manner because all the possibilities had not been foreseen. An unadulterated exercise of the paranormal faculties could provide a more objective assessment in which one might well see that the gratification of immediate personal aims would not be as advantageous as had been anticipated.

There is a similar reservation in respect of the prophetic dreams which are frequently experienced. A great deal of research has been devoted to the study of dreams both in respect of their physical nature and their psychological interpretation. It appears that during the normal sleep cycle there are two distinct phases. One is called orthodox sleep, during which the brain is largely quiescent, being primarily occupied with directing physiological restorative activities—a kind of recharging of the batteries. During the second phase, known as paradoxical sleep, the brain is partially aroused, and dreaming takes place. This phase is accompanied by curious rapid movements of the eyes, even though the eyelids remain closed, and if a subject is awakened during these periods he is found to have been dreaming, though if not awakened he often does not remember these dreams. Moreover, it seems that this REM (rapid-eye-movement) phase is essential to the maintenance of a healthy condition, so that every normal person dreams, without necessarily having been aware of the fact.

Now if one relates this to the concept of the brain as an interpretive mechanism it would seem that during orthodox sleep the many programmes required during the normal waking state are disconnected. However, when the brain has been physically refreshed, some of these again come into play; but because they are not provided with the full quota of information, they produce incorrect and imaginative interpretations, particularly in respect of the numerous anxiety programmes retained from the previous day. These should be cancelled every night—a process technically called clearing the computer—but because this is not done we experience a variety of 'worry dreams', some of sufficient intensity to be remembered when we wake.

Nevertheless the release of the brain from its customary duties permits it to respond to vestigial programmes laid down by the deeper levels of the mind which can explore parts of the Eternal fabric free from the restrictions of the ordinary level of consciousness. This can produce dreams of a clairvoyant quality, sometimes of a prophetic character but often of greater significance in respect of one's psychological state. But because in the ordinary way the brain does not understand the language of paranormal information, it interprets it in a garbled mixture of past associations and future tendencies, which may convey little meaning.[26]

The chances of intelligible interpretation of such dreams—and the ability to remember them on awakening—are evidently increased if the brain is free from unnecessary clutter. This is not necessarily confined to periods of sleep but can be contrived during waking periods if the necessary relaxation can be cultivated, thereby permitting the development of the latent paranormal sensitivity.

CHAPTER SIX

The Directing Intelligences

We sometimes speak of some achievement as being a miracle of organization. Only rarely do we recognize that this applies, quite literally, to the world in which we live. We rely on the fact that it appears, in general, to be an ordered structure; so that, for example, we confidently expect the sun to rise every day—though legend says that there have been occasions when it did not. Natural phenomena have been observed in great detail, with the consequent discovery of many of their patterns, all of which are assumed to have developed by accident. A more conscious awareness interprets this behaviour as the implementation of an organized plan, directed by intelligences of a superior order. This idea has already been discussed in general terms, but should now be examined more specifically.

It is a fundamental characteristic of the phenomenal world —the world of appearances interpreted by the senses—that its behaviour is dependent upon patterns of response to stimulus. We saw in Chapter 2 that this is the mechanism of the human senses which convert the impressions received from the environment into electrical signals which are then interpreted by the brain to provide the appropriate response. What is less generally appreciated in our egregious egotism is that all Nature is equipped with similar sensing equipment. These 'natural' senses do not necessarily operate in the same manner as the human senses, but the mechanism is the same in that the information which they provide is referred to some form of established programme which determines the appropriate response.

For example, plants convert the energy of sunlight into physical matter in the form of starch, which is itself a remarkable feat of chemistry, and by similarly sophisticated operations this is co-ordinated with other influences to produce growth. Moreover, this is only a small part of the overall pattern. Organic life responds to many other rhythms, by no means confined to the alternations of light and darkness. There are lunar rhythms, variations of magnetic field, and other influences which create stimuli of many kinds.

Even inanimate matter behaves in accordance with specific programmes. The various chemical elements will only combine in certain clearly-defined ways with which the extraordinary manipulations of modern chemistry have to conform. All physical behaviour, in fact, is conditioned by established patterns of response to stimulus.

* * *

What co-ordinates these operations? In the higher orders of the animal kingdom, including man, the impressions of the environment are converted by the senses into electrical signals which are then conveyed to the brain through a system of nerves, long cable-like assemblies of cells along which the impulses are transmitted from cell to cell. In this way the brain is provided with the data which it then analyses in accordance with previously established programmes.

Plants and primitive animals do not possess a nervous system. Their behaviour appears to depend upon some form of cellular communication, apparently chemical in character, which operates in an intelligent manner and yet is not directed by any localized centre corresponding to the brain of the higher orders.

One of the simplest forms of life is the amoeba, virtually a single cell having a variable and indeterminate shape, which exists by surrounding and engulfing small particles of food. It clearly possesses some rudimentary sense mechanism which it interprets within itself. Higher orders involve colonies of cells directed by a group intelligence which is not contained within the individual cells. This will lay down the programmes to which the colony conforms, so that it constitutes what may be called the *group mind* of the species.

There is ample evidence of this superior direction, which is clearly of an extra-physical character. For example, there is a small freshwater organism called Hydra, a parasite which attaches itself to water weeds. It is a well organized structure having a short pillar-like body with a series of tentacles. Samples of this organism can be completely pulverized to create an amorphous mixture known to biologists as Hydra soup, containing a mass of isolated and undifferentiated cells. Yet if this is left alone for a time these cells will integrate themselves into complete organisms again under the direction of their group mind.

Higher in the scale are plants, which are more elaborate structures having greater potentiality and purpose. They comprise a variety of specialized groups of cells each performing a specific function. The individual cells respond to the stimuli of their environment, such as light and warmth, and absorb nutrients of various kinds. To this extent they possess an intelligence, which is built into their design. As part of this intention they multiply by what is called mitosis, each cell dividing into two, and these again into two, and so on. This is the normal process of growth, which is not unrestrained but is controlled by the available energy intake. Yet at appropriate stages in the operation there is a differentiation involving the creation of new groups of specialized cells in the development from seed to leaf, to flower, to fruit. The biochemistry of the processes is well known, but this is no more than the mechanism. There is no evidence to suggest that the original cells contain within themselves the intelligence to interpret their information differently in the successive stages of growth.

There is clearly a directing intelligence of a superior order similar to that which Sir Charles Sherrington envisaged in the development of the human embryo discussed in Chapter 12.[31] One can postulate that each cell, or group of cells, fulfils its appointed role under the direction of the group mind of the species.

If we extend this concept we find further evidence of group intelligence in the phenomenal world. One of the most serious limitations of the conventional senses is their fragmentary interpretation of the impressions which they receive. For example, we see a flock of birds wheeling in the sky. The senses interpret this as an assembly of separate birds, whereas in reality the whole flock is an entity responding to the diredtion of a group mind. This is why they move in unison. The sensory impressions received by the individual birds, recording their height, direction of motion, distance from each other, and so forth, are co-ordinated in their brains in accordance with an established programme, which is just one of a whole range of behaviour patterns laid down by the group mind of the particular species. Other kinds of bird will have different programmes, some shared, some individual, but all created by the over-riding intelligence of the group mind of birds.

This group intelligence is particularly observed in insect colonies such as bees and ants in which concerted and often almost instant action is directed by an authority which is not vested in any single individual. There is a record of a colony of ants on the march which encountered a crevasse too deep to be crossed. In a very short time the leading ants formed themselves into a chain along the edge of the crevasse, and then swung this like a hinge to form a bridge over which the remainder of the marchers reached the other side.

Anyone who has seen a hornet's nest cannot fail to be impressed by the evidence of group intelligence. It is shaped like a rugby football containing internally a number of platforms made up of hexagonal cells, supported at appropriate points by pillars; all of which is constructed from fibrous material laboriously masticated by the workers. How do they know how to build this extraordinary edifice?

How does a spider know from the moment of its birth how to spin its elegantly precise web? There is no instruction or experience on which to rely, nor any process of trial and error; and although it has been suggested that certain physical influences, such as magnetic fields, may serve as references, this is no more than the mechanism of an operation directed by an extra-sensory intelligence. Whately Carrington, a leading exponent of parapsychology, has suggested that instinctive behaviour of this high order may be due to the individual spider being linked with a larger system in which is stored all the web-spinning experience of the whole species.

The concept of group mind provides a practical basis for the implementation of this extra-sensory rapport. Since it operates within the fabric of the real world, it will be aware of all the time-bodies of its species; and if some of these develop new techniques the information is instantly available to the remainder without having to pass through successive generations. An example of this is the rapidity with which blue tits throughout Western Europe have learned to peck off the tops of milk bottles.

* * *

There is a good deal of loose thinking about the mind, partly because of a certain poverty of language in respect of the immaterial aspects of man. Science now admits the existence of some directing intelligence. The eminent professor, Sir Cyril Burt, has indeed said that 'in a purely mechanical world . . . no phenomenon could possibly appear without some appropriate cause'. All too often, however, this is regarded as an extension of the physical realm, whereas it is really an exercise of a superior order of intelligence.

A further limitation of conventional thinking is that the mind is generally regarded as an exclusive prerogative of man, which is a lamentably arrogant assumption. Actually the behaviour of the whole physical world is directed by a variety of minds, not necessarily individual, all operating within the control of a superior Cosmic Intelligence.

Mind has been defined as the seat of consciousness, though I believe it can be better understood as an *instrument* of consciousness, which directs the physical mechanisms for which it is responsible.[26] This clearly implies intelligence, literally the ability to recognize relative connections, but this must be understood as operating at different levels. The mechanisms themselves necessarily have their own intelligence which enables them to make appropriate assessments of the information at their disposal; but the intelligence of the mind must be of a higher order than that of the mechanisms which it controls, being an interpretation of the superior relationships which exist in the real world.

The mind should therefore be regarded as exercising a *directing* intelligence, by virtue of its existence in the unmanifest realm of real causes discussed in Chapter 3. Moreover, because this realm is permeated by a variety of forms and levels of consciousness there must be a corresponding structure of separate minds concerned with the specific implementation of the several requirements. This is an idea of considerable potentiality which provides a much greater understanding of observed phenomena than is possible from a purely mechanistic view.

As a part—but only a part—of this structure there exists the human mind, which has the unique distinction of being individual. Moreover it can operate itself at different levels, which is why it can provide interpretations of a superior quality beyond conventional limitations. It is clearly not of a physical character because although the brain has a number of compartments concerned with the exercise of specific functions, these are only parts of the mechanism. Each is highly intelligent in its own sphere, but they are all subject to the direction of a superior intelligence which does not reside in the physical body. It is actually a composite structure containing subdivisions responsible for the direction of the physical, emotional and intellectual functions respectively.[21, 26]

The human mind, indeed, is a structure of magnificent potentiality which is discussed more fully in Chapter 17. It normally operates only at its most mechanical level which is (quite rightly) concerned with the interpretation of physical phenomena, but its higher levels respond to influences within the pattern of the real world which are created by superior levels of consciousness.

With these the paranormal faculty can communicate, though only to a limited extent because human understanding, even at its highest levels, is incommensurable with that of the Cosmic Mind. Nevertheless, it is possible to attain a partial comprehension of the underlying patterns and even, on occasion, to influence them to create miraculous changes of behaviour if these are considered appropriate.

* * *

The first step must clearly be to envisage in practical terms the manner in which the intelligences in the unmanifest realm direct the behaviour of the phenomenal world. Since the Universe is an ordered structure one can postulate a chain of authority in which the overall direction is exercised through a variety of subordinate minds concerned with detailed manifestations. These are not only concerned with living matter, but also operate in the inorganic realm. For the present, however, let us look broadly at the structure of organic life, starting with the kingdom of plant life.

This is apt to be taken for granted, though it plays a vital part in the scheme, for without it we could not survive. Apart from their value as food for organic life, plants have an essential role in the replenishment of the earth's resources. By the process known as photosynthesis they convert the energy of sunlight into physical matter (which is why they grow, for plant growth is not entirely, or even mainly, dependent on nourishment from the soil). They do this by means of plastids, one type of which contains chlorophyll, which has the green colour characteristic of vegetation. In the process they absorb a variety of simple compounds from the atmosphere, mainly carbon dioxide, water vapour and nitrogen, and give off oxygen, so replenishing the supply of this vital constituent. It has been calculated that the total

THE DIRECTING INTELLIGENCES

mass of free oxygen in the air—some 10,000 billion tons—is equal to the total mass of living matter on the earth's surface.

This balance is maintained by the operation of natural laws. Vegetation multiplies at a prodigious rate, as is evidenced by the rapid growth of weeds in waste land, and except in hostile environment such as deserts, quickly occupies all the available space. Certain forms, such as trees, have learned to find extra space by growing upwards, and even simple grasses develop folded leaves to increase their rigidity, so finding extra room.

But there are other natural balances, notably in the world of insects which are directed by a different group mind. These multiply at such a rate that if they were not checked by predators they would over-run the globe in the space of a few years. Even more dramatic are the bacteria, many of which are useful, but which multiply so progidiously that they would cover the earth in 36 hours were it not for the limited supply of dissolved gases in the media in which they live, and which they need to breathe. This again is a limitation imposed by the group mind of the species, subservient to a higher intelligence.

The higher the organism the more space it needs. Duckweed requires only the space of its own cells, so that it rapidly covers the surface of a pond, and is then checked. Birds and mammals require more room and the size of their colonies is adapted to the available space. Throughout the world the conditions adjust themselves so that the overall geochemical energy expended in the maintenance of life is just equal to the intake of energy from the Sun.

There is a further balance which is not so obvious. Not all the energy from the Sun is beneficial. There is a high proportion of ultra-violet radiation which is inimical to life, but this is fortunately unable to penetrate the outer atmosphere. On the other hand there are benign radiations, such as heat, which do reach the earth, but which in the absence of vegetation would be uselessly reflected. These and other energies are absorbed by living matter and re-radiated in a modified form which is trapped by the air. Hence the atmosphere serves the double duty of shielding us from harmful radiations and retaining the essential warmth; but to do this effectively its constitution and quantity must be preserved within suitable limits, in which process organic life plays an important part.

This delicately-balanced structure can be regarded as having resulted from a fortunate concatenation of accidents, in which man himself is a similarly accidental development. It seems more intelligent to concede the possibility of a controlling mind.

* * *

The Universe is not designed solely for the benefit of man. Swedenborg maintained that the place of everything in the scheme of things was determined by its use, and we can envisage that the Cosmic Mind in fulfilment of its purposes created subsidiary minds charged with the development of the multiplicity of component entities throughout all organic life.

Vitus B. Droscher, in his book *The Friendly Beast* (W. H. Allen), discusses a variety of patterns of sociology in animal behaviour which contain clear evidence of directing intelligence—patterns which, he says, man has outgrown to his detriment.

The idea of a directing Intelligence, indeed, is modifying the earlier rigid doctrines of evolution. As Sir Alister Hardy has said in a Symposium entitled *Science and E.S.P.*[8] 'if something akin to telepathy . . . was found to be a factor in moulding the patterns of behaviour among members of a species . . . it might operate through organic selection to modify the course of evolution'. It is, in fact, no longer necessary, nor even fashionable, to reject the concept of an intelligent Universe, and since this must be an essentially ordered structure one can postulate that evolutionary processes will make use of the appropriate laws of the phenomenal world as the most convenient way of implementing the creative design.

CHAPTER SEVEN

The Sensitivity of Plants

In our preoccupation with our imagined destiny as lords of creation we have only a perfunctory consideration for the presumed lower orders. There is a certain respect for animals, perhaps because their behaviour is in many respects similar to our own, but the attitude is usually one of tolerant (or sometimes aggressive) superiority, which is stupidly arrogant. Animals in general do not possess an individual mind and hence have only a rudimentary intellect. They have a mechanical memory which sometimes gives the impression of reasoning, but this is not a true intellectual faculty, which is not necessary for their purpose in the scheme. On the other hand, by virtue of their group intelligence they possess a certain natural extra-sensory cognition, whereas in man this has to be cultivated.

It is well known that animals respond readily to emotional atmosphere, even among themselves. Pigs, for example, flourish better in company rather than isolation. More significant is the response to human affection. I am not referring to sentimental attachment which is interpreted by the animal (and its owner) in terms of purely sensual comfort. The genuine animal-lover exercises an impersonal understanding which creates a wordless rapport of surprising depth. Conversely, there is a marked reaction to negative states, such as fear. It is sometimes suggested that this arises from some odour which is given off in a state of anxiety—not necessarily exclusively by human beings; but if so, it is no more than the physical interpretation of a lack of harmony in the underlying (unmanifest) patterns.

Moreover, there is the known reaction of animals to evil environments. A typical example is the experience of a former colleague of mine who was riding a horse through the outback of Australia. At a certain place his horse repeatedly refused to go on, and he subsequently discovered that this had been the scene of a particularly brutal murder. There are many instances of the ability of dogs to 'scent' danger, and to display other forms of super-sensory understanding. The evidence of rapport between human beings and animals, in fact, is so widespread that it is taken for granted, and disregarded as unimportant, whereas it is really a clear indication of the existence of a higher order of intelligence with which our puny self-interest does not communicate.

* * *

Our attitude to plants is even more insensitive. They are not, as a rule, regarded as sentient beings. Yet as long ago as 1906 the celebrated Indian scientist, Sir Jagadis Chunder Bose, demonstrated by delicate measuring equipment that plants had feelings similar to those exhibited by higher organisms. His work was far ahead of its time, but it has since been confirmed in a dramatic fashion by the experiments of Cleve Backster, an American psychologist who had frequent occasion in his work to use a polygraph or 'lie detector'. This is an instrument which measures the electrical resistance of the skin, which has been found to vary significantly with emotional stress. If one is asked a question to which one does not wish to give a truthful answer, the emotional conflict produces a momentary change in the conductivity of, say, the palm of the hand, which can be recorded on a chart.

One day Backster was about to water a potted rubber plant in his office when it occurred to him that by attaching his polygraph to one of the leaves he might be able to detect changes in the surface resistance and so to estimate the time taken for the moisture to rise from the roots. The results were inconclusive in this respect, but he found to his surprise that the polygraph record began to show a pattern similar to that exhibited by a human being subject to a momentary emotional stimulus.

Now it is an established technique in polygraph work to trigger emotional reactions for test purposes by a threat to the well-being of the subject. He therefore decided to apply this to the plant. Immersing one of the leaves in a cup of hot coffee had no effect, so he decided to burn the leaf with a match. At the instant of making this decision there was a dramatic response from the polygraph, though he had not approached the plant or actually carried out his intention in any way. He concluded that the plant had in some way actually read his mind!

He continued his experiments with remarkable results. Similar effects were observed with other plants, which were confirmed by other investigators. He found also that plants responded (differently) to benign influences, and that one plant, a Philodendron, appeared to have a particularly happy relationship with him. Hence in experiments on this plant he used his assistant to pose the threats, with the result that after a time the plant cringed whenever his assistant came into the room, but relaxed if Backster himself approached, or even spoke in an adjoining room.

In another experiment he brought some live shrimps into the room in which there was a plant with a polygraph attached. He then employed a machine to kill the shrimps at random intervals by dropping them one by one into boiling water, with no human being present in the room. At each death the plant exhibited a violent reaction—an effect similar to that of the rabbits in the submarine mentioned in Chapter 5. Yet if the machine dropped in a shrimp which was already dead the plant took no notice.

Another group of investigators headed by Aristide Esser, a psychiatrist at a New York hospital, interviewed a woman with a plant which she had raised and nurtured with affection. They attached a polygraph to the plant, and asked her a variety of questions, some of which she answered untruthfully. In every such case the plant responded as if the polygraph had been attached to the woman herself.

* * *

These experiments are of more than superficial significance. They provide a clear indication of some form of extra-physical intelligence which operates throughout the vegetable kingdom, and which can assist our understanding of the overall direction of the phenomenal world. The work of Bose and others has confirmed that plants are sentient organisms, but such senses as they possess do not operate in the conventional manner. The individual cells respond to stimuli of various kinds and there is some communication between the adjacent cells of the structure, which appears to be of a chemical nature, but there is no nervous system whereby information can be conveyed to a physical co-ordinating centre.

Yet plants exhibit a clear awareness of themselves as a whole. For example, a Mimosa is very sensitive to touch, and if one leaf is crushed the whole plant wilts in sympathy. In the absence of a physical co-ordinating system one would expect any cellular communication to be purely localized, yet there appears to be some overall intelligence in operation. Again, plants have been shown to be sensitive to sounds, flourishing if these are harmonious, such as one of Bach's Brandenburg Concertos, but reacting adversely to cacophony —influences which affect the plant as a whole, and not just the individual cells.

There is the discrimination mentioned earlier whereby the cells develop differently in the successive stages of growth. One of the fascinating aspects of Nature is its astonishing variety. What determines the difference between a rose and a cabbage, or between a wayside flower and an oak tree? Why does a juniper always grow upright, while a fruit tree adopts a spreading form? The botanist will say that the differences arise from appropriate variations in the genetic code contained in the nuclei of the cells, stemming from some accidental mutation in the remote past which set them on their differing evolutionary paths.

Yet each has a specific usefulness in the pattern of organic life which is directed by an intelligence of a higher order. A plant, indeed, has a certain awareness of its destiny. Its day-to-day appearance is only a cross-section in time of its 'long body' in Eternity, so that its physical growth can be seen as filling a shape which has already been allotted to it by the direction of the group mind of its particular species. The differing gene structures are merely the mechanism by which the requirements of this directing intelligence are implemented.

Within this framework one can understand that since these intelligences operate within the unmanifest realm they are susceptible to other influences operating at the same level. We have seen that all physical happenings are interpretations of a pattern in the real world, in which they leave a continuing trace called the time-body. These many time-bodies are interwoven in the fabric of Eternity and so do not exist in isolation but are mutually inter-dependent. In particular, the emotions or intentions of a human being will be incorporated into his or her time-body, and this can influence the time-body of a plant which is at the time in close relationship. Hence the extra-sensory rapport observed by Backster and his associates is really an entirely natural phenomenon, but one which we are normally too engrossed in self-interest to recognize.

* * *

The rapport between humans and plants is not necessarily hostile, and is often quite the reverse. It is well known that some people are said to have 'green fingers' so that plants in their care flourish to an unusual degree. This is, quite simply, the result of a sub-conscious awareness of the plant as a living being, existing in its own right. This creates a relationship to which the plant responds, recognizing the implied good will, which is often actually expressed in words. There is an appreciation of the effort which the plant is making, and perhaps the beauty of its flowers, which is not taken for granted but is an occasion for mutual rejoicing.

If this sounds sentimental, pause to reflect how rarely one gives thanks to the Universe. Without this there can be no magic. To dictate to a plant will have no effect, but to communicate with it as a fellow being can produce a positive response. This has been strikingly demonstrated by an experiment at Findhorn in the north of Scotland. Here a small community established itself in a somewhat barren locality with the object of practising a more conscious way of life, in the course of which they developed an entirely inhospitable territory into a garden of flourishing profusion. This was accomplished by conscious communication with the group mind of the flowers and vegetables, which responded to the affection in a quite remarkable way.

This extra-sensory rapport is not confined to plants. It operates equally within the animal kingdom, as has been illustrated earlier, and even in the inanimate realm. It is, in fact, a natural exercise of paranormal faculties which, in man, are very indifferently developed.

* * *

The discovery that plants are sentient organisms which react to any threat to their life has prompted speculation about the pain which may be occasioned by their destruction or damage in the ordinary course of events. Is the popular song of an earlier generation—Don't be cruel to a vegetabule—not so facetious after all? There is a certain amount of confused, and even sentimental, opinion about this, and the matter must be viewed in its proper perspective.

Everything in the Universe is eaten by something of a higher order, either physically or psychologically, in the course of which a certain quality of energy is released, which serves a cosmic purpose. Part of the function of vegetable matter is to provide food for animals and humans, so that within the intelligence of organic life plants are aware of their place and purpose. If they are killed in pursuance of their destiny the pain is acceptable, and makes some kind of contribution to the overall system. Hence if one is aware of Nature as a living organism there can be an element of request in one's actions—even in such simple matters as mowing a lawn or picking a flower—and permission is gladly given. My lawn, indeed, may become the more luxuriant, or my vegetables or fruit appreciably more tasty.

This is quite different from wanton destruction, at which man is only too adept—not by any means only in respect of plant life—and this causes unnecessary suffering which the Universe does not need, and which only disturbs the essential harmony. We need not elaborate this here, save to note that this imbalance is responsible for the evils of modern society, with which mankind has to contend while it is learning to grow up psychologically.

CHAPTER EIGHT

Before your very eyes!

In the treacherous world of everyday life the one thing we regard as certain is that the familiar objects of our surroundings will continue to exist. Even if, as we are told, they are illusions of the senses, they have an established and practical reality with which we have to live. Yet we have seen that the world contains exciting possibilities which are not superficially apparent, so that it is worth while to try to understand how the familiar structures are assembled.

Actually, the perceptions of the senses are illusory on two counts. Firstly, because they only provide a limited representation of conditions which to a different range of senses would not appear the same; but more significantly because these appearances are merely transitory interpretations of a pattern which does not exist at the phenomenal level. We saw earlier (in Chapter 3) that the word phenomenal means 'coming into being', so that all physical objects should be regarded as being continuously brought into existence by the reactions of the senses. This is a novel and perhaps startling idea. Yet it is corroborated by a variety of scientific evidence, and has a number of practical implications.

Before discussing this, however, let us look briefly at what science tells us of the patterns of the physical world. It is a magical structure, full of remarkable transformations, most of which are usually taken entirely for granted. Consider, for example, that familiar substance, water. If we heat it, it disappears—as when a kettle boils dry. If we cool it sufficiently it turns into a solid (ice). Moreover water itself is composed, chemically, of two invisible gases, hydrogen and oxygen, Bring them together under suitable conditions and they combine to form a liquid. There are countless other transformations continually taking place in the natural world, which ought to arouse a sense of wonder, but rarely do.

Various attempts have been made over the years to explain these effects. There was even a crude atomic theory propounded by Empedocles in 400 B.C., his 'atom' being the smallest particle of a substance which retained its individuality, but it was not until some 2,000 years later that coherent theories began to be formulated based on experimental evidence. The first real advance was made by the British scientist, John Dalton, who found that different chemical substances always combined in the same proportions. This led him to the belief that all natural substances were themselves compounds of basic materials which he called elements. He showed, for example, that common salt is a combination of a light metal called sodium and a poisonous gas called chlorine. Yet the two will combine to provide the quite different and savoury white crystals of common salt.

Based on these investigations he put forward, in 1803, his atomic theory which first introduced the concept of the atom as we know it today. The term 'atom' he applied only to the elements, which chemically were indivisible, and he suggested that all chemical substances were formed by combinations of certain elements which had a natural affinity for each other; he called these *molecules*.

Pursuing this theory science soon discovered many new elements beyond the 20-odd of his time, and today there are over 100 known elements, mostly natural, but some artificially created by nuclear physicists. Moreover, molecular structure has been found to apply not only to inorganic material, but to living matter, the cells of which contain long chain-like molecules in which a small number of basic elements are assembled in a repeating pattern.

For a long time, however, the reasons for this behaviour were not understood until it was discovered that atoms were not, in fact, the ultimate particles. At the beginning of the

THE AGE OF MIRACLES

present century, J. J. Thomson's researches in electricity led him to suggest that electric currents, and electrical effects in general, were produced by minute particles nearly 2,000 times lighter than the smallest atom, the hydrogen atom. Moreover the evidence suggested that these minute electrical particles, which he called electrons, were in some way constituent parts of the atoms themselves.

This led the Danish scientist Niels Bohr, then a young student at Manchester University, to put forward, in 1909, the theory of the nuclear atom which is the basis of modern ideas. According to this theory the atom is composed of a central nucleus which carries a positive electrical charge, around which revolves a series of negatively-charged electrons, each in its own orbit, as illustrated in Fig. 7.

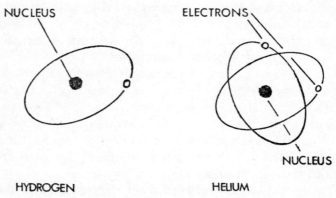

FIG. 7 Simple atomic structure

The dimensions of these atoms are fantastically small. For example, the estimated weight of a hydrogen atom is $1 \cdot 66 \times 10^{-24}$ grams. This is a mathematical shorthand denoting that the figure 1·66 must be divided by the figure 1 followed by 24 noughts—i.e. one million million million million. Expressed in another way, one gram of hydrogen (approximately 1/30th of an ounce) contains approximately 600,000 million million million atoms!

The difference between the various elements is determined simply by the number of electrons within the atom. Hydrogen, the lightest element, contains only one electron. Lead, which is nearly the heaviest, contains 82. Beyond this number the orbits tend to become unstable and the nucleus cannot hold on to the outermost electrons, which escape from time to time and give rise to the phenomenon known as radio-activity.

Now these discoveries have one implication of enormous significance. If the electron has only 1/2,000th the mass of even the lightest element, the atom must be made up mostly of empty space—empty, that is, in terms of material. It forms, in fact, a miniature solar system. By numerous experiments of the most delicate and ingenious nature, physicists have established that this is indeed the case and that the world of the atom is a replica in miniature of the macrocosm of the heavenly bodies.

The nucleus of the atom—the 'sun' around which the electrons revolve—has a diameter about 1/100,000th of the atom and the electrons are even more minute. These figures are approximate since the atoms themselves vary in size, but it is clear that the relative spaces within the atoms are enormous. Eddington likened the electrons in an atom to a few specks of dust floating in the relative immensity of Waterloo Station.

We see objects because the electromagnetic vibrations to which our eyes have been designed to respond, which we call light, produce certain kinds of interference with the internal forces binding the atoms together, so that some objects appear visible and others, like the wind, invisible. Objects appear hard or soft, hot or cold, to our sense of touch because of the interaction of the invisible forces between the atoms of our fingers and those of the object. Our whole awareness of the physical world is based on these interactions registered by the senses, which provide a practical relationship to a pattern which is really of an entirely different nature.

It is in this unmanifest realm that the real intelligence

operates, so that it is unnecessary for the present purpose to pursue in detail the manifestations at the phenomenal level. The physical structures disclose clear evidence of superior design, particularly in the table of elements discussed in the Appendix, and in general they conform to consistent laws which science can interpret in terms of atoms and electrons—to which it has now added a bewildering array of sub-nuclear particles. The use of these concepts has permitted the astonishing developments of modern civilization, but none of this expertise has any *absolute* reality, being based on interpretations which are primarily an exercise of sense-based intelligence.

* * *

In contrast to these theories, the ancients regarded the Universe as being composed of only four elements—Fire, Air, Water and Earth. This is customarily dismissed as a survival from the supposedly ignorant dawn of civilization, but the concept is actually of much more real validity. Plato saw the world of matter as having devolved from a higher spiritual realm, so that the four elements of ancient cosmology are not physical substances but relate to successively denser manifestations of reality. This accords with the concept of a superior realm in which lie the causes of phenomenal manifestations, so that it is possible to envisage that the substances of the physical world are being continuously created out of the material of the unmanifest world.

Some such effect is evidently present in the process of photosynthesis in plants which was first investigated some hundred years ago by Baron von Herzeels of Hanover. By a large number of experiments he established that plants during their growth acquired in some way substances which were not present in either their nutrients or in the air which they breathed. Today this is explained in physical terms as resulting from the transformation of the energy of sunlight into material substance as part of the natural operations of the phenomenal world.

However, this seems an over-facile interpretation for there are aspects of the process which suggest the influence of a directing intelligence. For example, in one experiment plants grown in a phosphorus solution were found to absorb phosphorus from the solution (which accordingly showed a diminution in its phosphorus content). Yet they did not themselves exhibit any increase in phosphorus in their tissues, but there was an increase in their *sulphur* content, indicating that they had made sulphur out of phosphorus. As shown in the Appendix, this is one of the stages in the evolution of the chemical series, the interesting point being that plants are apparently able to achieve this transmutation as part of their natural programme.

Little remains of von Herzeel's work, which was ahead of its time, but his experiments have been repeated and extended in recent years by the German scientist Rudolf Hauschka, who not only verified the earlier findings but discovered a series of remarkable rhythms. For example, he found that during the period of the waxing moon, the weight of plants increased, indicating the creation of matter by photosynthesis, but during the subsequent waning period the weight decreased to its original value.

From these and other experiments, which are recorded in a fascinating book entitled *The Nature of Substance*,[9] he suggests that there is a rhythmic crystallization and 're-etherialization' of matter from the real world due to extra-terrestrial influences. Matter, he suggests, is the *precipitate* of life, created by the continuous translation of the immaterial essence into material form.

* * *

In pursuance of this idea one can postulate that all physical matter is brought into being by a progressive assembly of its basic constituents. The chemical elements, for example, are known to conform to a pattern which evolves progressively from the simplest to the most complex by the successive incorporation of additional electrons in the structure. The significant feature is that each of these stages involves a specific increase in energy, so that there is a progressive development in the pattern; but whereas this is ordinarily regarded as having happened in the past, there is reason to believe that it is a continuing process. Astronomers suggest, indeed, that matter is being continuously created in the stars out of the intangible fabric of the universe.

However, this still implies that the successive stages, once created, remain in existence. Yet it is an established fact that everything in the physical world only has a limited lifetime. Man, for example, lives for about 80 years on average. Yet the cells of his body die every few days and have to be replaced (except the brain cells which live throughout his life). We do not have clear information about the life of atoms, but we do know that the constituent electrons appear to have a very brief existence. Certainly one can never say 'there is an electron here', but only that there is evidence of its existence a moment ago. Some of the hypothetical sub-nuclear particles are calculated to have lifetimes of a few billionths of a second.

There must clearly be a mechanism of continual replenishment. In the cells of the body this can be regarded as an operation of the general laws of living matter, but there is no known mechanism relating to atoms and electrons. Yet replenishment there must be or the physical world would simply disappear, but because of this continuous replacement of the wastage the senses do not register any discontinuity and create the illusion of a steady state.

We experience this kind of illusion in the pictures on our T.V. or cinema screens, which appear to be continuous but are actually a succession of separate images which are repeated too rapidly for the eyes to distinguish. By analogy, one can suppose that every phenomenal manifestation is produced by the creation of a specific quantum of energy which will not persist indefinitely but will be dissipated in the fulfilment of its particular function and will then need to be renewed. This will apply throughout the physical world, every constituent of which is created in its own time-scale by its appropriate directing intelligence in the unmanifest realm.

This will develop in a co-ordinated structure of increasing complexity. From the material of the sub-atomic particles, created and maintained by their group intelligence, there will be assemblies of atoms directed by an intelligence of a coarser order. This in turn will be followed by molecular structures, first of inorganic material and then by the elaborate structures of living matter, each stage having its appropriate lifetime, replenished by further injections of the appropriate energy.

The details of the process are not detected by the ordinary senses, which regard everything as having a continuing existence. Nor is it necessary for them to react otherwise, since their interpretations are entirely adequate for the normal purposes of life. But one can postulate that a higher level of awareness, such as is exercised by the paranormal senses, can communicate with the intelligences of the successive creative stages, and can modify the established patterns temporarily or permanently, so producing a miracle.

* * *

A similar idea was put forward in the early years of the present century by the distinguished physician J. E. R. McDonagh, F.R.C.S., who had been seeking to discover the basic causes of disease, and came to the conclusion that every malady was caused by an imbalance of the protein in the blood. This he attributed to some derangement of the mechanism by which this protein was being produced.[17]

Pursuing this line of thought he postulated a process of continuous creation out of the primordial unmanifest structure. This he suggested operated in a succession of pulsating rhythms, which resulted in the manifestation first of the sub-atomic particles, followed by their integration first into atoms, and then into the molecules and crystals of inorganic matter. At this stage a different quality of (vital) energy is injected resulting in the creation of amino-acids and proteins, followed by the integration of these materials into the tissues of the vegetable and animal kingdoms.

He contended that if some malign influence disturbed the proper creation of the protein, this affected the subsequent stages and so caused illness. His ideas were rejected in his generation as too unorthodox, but it has since been established that it is possible, by the use of dowsing, actually to communicate with the protein during its creative stage and correct any disturbances at this level. This has resulted in a new technique of medicine which has produced remarkable results, and is discussed in Chapter 12.

* * *

It seems that the concept of continuous creation can provide an insight into the mechanism of a wide variety of supernatural phenomena. In spiritual healing, for example, one can envisage that the actual creation of the cells of the body is modified. Moreover since this is a continuous process the effect can be virtually instantaneous, whereas any operations at physical level must be inordinately slower. The influence of thought over the physical behaviour of plants discussed in the previous chapter can be interpreted in similar terms, as also can many other supernatural effects.

In practical terms it can be understood that the creative patterns are not concerned only with the initiation of the particular entity, but will direct its subsequent behaviour. If the pattern is modified, the physical manifestations will also depart from the norm, and these departures may be detected by conventional methods. Hence there can be tangible evidence of the happening as a change in the physical reactions or even the structure, but these must be recognized as the effect and not the cause.

Nor is this mechanism applicable only to living matter. So-called inanimate objects are continuously brought into being in a similar way by an appropriate sequence of creative intelligences (prior to the injection of vital energy). These also can be over-ridden by the direction of a higher level of consciousness. We cited in Chapter 4 the control of natural forces exercised by the Kahunas, and there are many other examples of the control of 'mind over matter' which parapsychologists call psychokinesis or P.K. Many people possess an inherent ability to produce such effects, often without being aware that they are responsible; nor are they necessarily the result of human agency.

CHAPTER NINE

Planetary Influences

It is an age-old tradition that the course of events is influenced by the stars, and the ancient art of astrology was concerned with the study and application of these influences. However, this was superseded by the more precise science of astronomy devoted to the study of the physical behaviour of the heavenly bodies, which disclosed a structure of such unimaginable vastness that the earth, and still more its puny denizens, appeared utterly insignificant. Hence any suggestion that man's individual fortunes could be influenced by this majestic structure was treated with derision.

Today a less rigid attitude prevails, for biological research has shown that the whole of organic life, and even the earth itself, is influenced by a variety of rhythms, most of which are of extra-terrestrial origin. Hence the world does not exist in isolation, but this must be interpreted in its proper scale and context. The mass horoscopes in the popular press, which purport to forecast favourable trends for all people born under certain signs of the Zodiac, merely pander to public credulity, and are not to be taken seriously. On the other hand an individual and objective assessment may indicate relationships in the real world which can be of significance.

Let us approach the subject more intelligently by considering first of all some of the observed rhythms in the natural world. The most obvious one is the alternation of light and darkness which we call a day. This is caused by the rotation of the earth on its axis, as a result of which each part of the globe in turn faces the Sun during its rotation and thereby receives its appropriate quota of the vital radiations of light and heat.

The hours of daylight vary with season and latitude, and there are other influences encountered during the period. Hence it is usual to refer to these cyclical variations as a *circadian* rhythm—a word coined by Franz Halberg meaning 'about a day'.

This regulates the behaviour of organic life in general, particularly in respect of the essential rhythm of waking and sleeping. This we take for granted, but without periodic rest the limited daily intake of energy would become too rapidly exhausted. We recognize this is our own everyday experience, but do not usually realize that the requirement applies throughout the whole of Nature.

We are familiar with the way many flowers open during the daytime and close at night. We know that plant life in general breathes in carbon dioxide by day and gives off oxygen when the Sun goes down. This is their rhythm of waking and sleeping, to which we usually give little thought. Yet it is essential to their survival, as was demonstrated by the American botanist W. S. Hillman in some experiments with tomato plants. He found that if these were kept under conditions of constant light and heat, the leaves wilted and died, but that the plants were quite healthy if there was a cyclic variation of temperature every 24 hours, which provided them with the opportunity to rest.

All organisms, in fact, require appropriate periods of recuperation if they are to survive, and this is provided by some form of circadian rhythm. There is, for example, a microscopic organism called Euglena which inhabits pond waters. This has a rudimentary photo-sensitive organ by which it orientates itself to light and moves about in search of food, but when the light fades it ceases to move and rests.

There are other rhythms in the circadian pattern to which Nature responds. For example, there is a member of the algae family called Volvox which is a small globular organism provided with cilia by which it propels itself through the water in a rolling motion in search of the most suitable conditions for the photosynthesis by which it lives. This movement is directed by the earth's magnetic field which varies slightly during the day, so that it moves in one direction in the morning and in the other in the afternoon; but when darkness falls it rests. Here is a subsidiary rhythm, which is also observed in certain other organisms as part of the experiments which Nature has made in the process of evolution.

A less obvious example of conformity to rhythm is the behaviour of the fruit fly, Drosophila, so popular with biologists because its rapid breeding cycle provides such excellent opportunities for experiment. Insects in general are equipped with a protective surface on their wings to prevent them from losing moisture too rapidly. However, fruit flies at birth have a very soft wing structure so that they need a humid atmosphere until their wings can harden. Hence they only emerge from their pupa cases at dawn, when the air is cool and moist.

These are but a few of the circadian patterns in organic life which are discussed in fascinating detail by Lyall Watson in his book Supernature.[88] They can hardly fail to arouse a keen sense of wonder at the intricacies of the natural world of which we are, for the most part, sublimely unaware.

* * *

Let us look briefly at some of the other influences in the natural world. Superposed on the diurnal rhythms which arise from the rotation of the earth there is a lunar rhythm derived from the transit of the moon, which has a slightly different period. It makes a complete orbit round the earth every 27·3 days, which means that any point on the surface of the globe takes slightly more than 24 hours to come opposite to a corresponding point on the moon, so that the lunar 'day' occupies 24·8 hours.

The most familiar effect of the moon's transit is the gravitational pull which it exerts on the oceans of the world, causing the cyclical ebb and flow of the tides. This occurs roughly once a day, but because of the slightly longer lunar rhythm, high tide is 48 minutes later each day. However, this is only one of the effects, for the moon influences organic life in many subtle ways.

The metabolism of plants has been shown to follow a lunar rhythm, and many people believe that they should be planted during a waxing moon. Old-wives' tales say that the efficacy of herbal remedies depends on the time in the lunar month when they are picked, and medical research has found that many orthodox remedies are more beneficial if they are taken during certain phases of the moon.

The influence on human behaviour is well known. People with psychotic tendencies are known to become more unstable when the moon is full, which is why in earlier times they were called lunatics, but even in normal circumstances there is a lunar rhythm in emotional activity. There is a correlation with the human menstrual period, for though this in general is not exact there is evidence which suggests that ovulation follows a lunar cycle.[38]

Marine organisms tend to adapt themselves to lunar rather than solar rhythms and regulate their behaviour in accordance with the rise and fall of the tides. Oysters, for example, open their shells during the periods of high water, but close them on the ebb. There are many other examples of response to the lunar influence which need not be discussed in detail. They are a part of the overall circadian rhythm of the natural world.

* * *

These effects can be regarded as a mechanical response to natural rhythms, consistent with the idea that all behaviour is determined by the response to stimuli detected by appropriate sensing mechanisms; but while this is true, there is an additional factor of considerable significance. Scientific investigation has shown that the various rhythms are innate in the organism and continue, at least for a time, if the external stimulus is absent.

The microscopic organism Euglena, for example, will continue for a time with its cycle of waking and sleeping even if kept in conditions of total darkness. In another experiment an American scientist, Frank Brown, removed some oysters from their natural habitat to a tank in his home in Illinois, one thousand miles away, and found that they went through the same cycles of opening and closing, as if they had still been in tidal waters.[4] This continued for 14 days, after which they abruptly changed their pattern to conform to a tidal rhythm which would apply to their new location one thousand miles west of their original situation.

Numerous other experiments have confirmed that living matter in general behaves in accordance with internal rhythms which are inherent in the organism but which are kept in step with external circadian (or other) rhythms by appropriate stimuli. This is a well-known scientific technique known as synchronization in which a system is allowed to develop, from its own resources, a rhythm which is approximately correct, but which is pulled into step at suitable intervals by a controlling influence. This makes a much more efficient use of the available energy.

This control is not confined to circadian rhythms, nor even to the simpler forms of life. Plants and animals (including man) all have their internal clocks which are controlled by cosmic influences of many kinds.[15] However, the question arises as to how these internal rhythms are laid down in the first place. Many of them are clearly not derived from experience. The fruit fly in its pupa stage has no experience of its forthcoming birth. How does it know precisely when to emerge? In any case, we have seen that the lower orders of life do not possess the analytical mechanism necessary to assess experience.

There is evidence here of the existence of group intelligences which direct the response to these natural rhythms, and a similar process can operate in respect of the longer-term rhythms to which plant and animal life respond, which will be discussed in a moment. In these terms one can envisage that the whole gamut of natural phenomena is no accident, but is directed by an intelligence of a superior order. Not only the internal rhythms, but the external controlling influences, are part of an integrated whole.

* * *

In addition to the relatively short-term circadian rhythms there are influences of a longer periodicity. There is, for example, the rhythm resulting from the annual orbit of the earth round the Sun. This creates, among other things, the changing seasons to which plants and animals respond in familiar ways. It is responsible for the patterns of migration in birds and hibernation in animals. Here again there is evidence that the patterns are innate, created by the group mind of the species. Kenneth Fisher, of the University of Toronto, kept some tiny ground squirrels in a windowless room at a constant temperature with a cycle of twelve hours light and twelve hours darkness every day. They remained healthy and active until October when they went into hibernation and awoke again in the following April—their normal cycle, despite the fact that there had been no climatic or other change in their environment.[23] It is unnecessary to discuss these patterns in detail, for it is clear that the whole phenomenal world is governed by a network of rhythms. What is significant is that all these rhythms are derived, fundamentally, from influences from outside the earth itself. However, there is no reason to suppose that the rhythms so far discussed are the only ones to which the earth is subject. It is equally likely that the transits of the planets will create rhythms which can affect the earth in unsuspected ways, and certainly the transit of the solar system through the galaxy, which completes its circuit in 25,800 years, must produce its own stupendous rhythm. We must examine the possibilities of these more remote celestial influences, which is the concern of the ancient art of astrology.

* * *

THE AGE OF MIRACLES

Popular science has familiarized us with the broad structure of the solar system containing a series of planets which travel round the Sun at increasing distances, as shown in Fig. 8. Many people, however, probably imagine that these planets, of which the earth is one, all rotate in unison whereas in fact each has its own period of orbit. Mercury, for example, makes just over four revolutions round the Sun during the Earth's year, while the outermost planet, Pluto, takes 248 earth years to complete its orbit. The different times, and distances, are as shown in Table 1.

TABLE 1 *The Planetary System*

Planet	Distance from sun (relative to earth)	Period of revolution (years)
Mercury	0.39	0.24
Venus	0.72	0.62
Earth	1	1
Mars	1.52	1.88
Jupiter	5.20	11.86
Saturn	9.54	29.46
Uranus	19.19	84.01
Neptune	30.07	164.78
Pluto	39.8	248

It will be obvious that any radiations or other influences which reach the earth from any of these planets will be subject to its own rhythm. Thus one might expect the influence of Venus, whatever it may be, to be a maximum every 7½ months of our time, though this is an over simplification because other factors are involved. Moreover, there will be periods when the influences of different planets reinforce or oppose each other. In astrological terms, they are said to be in conjunction, or in opposition, and since these continually changing relationships develop throughout the whole structure it is clear that the earth is subject to a wide variety of influences.

Moreover, these influences are themselves variable. The ancients, observing the heavenly firmament, interpreted it as a vast dome covering the earth, which they called the Zodiac, meaning a backcloth or painted scene. This they divided into

PLANETARY INFLUENCES

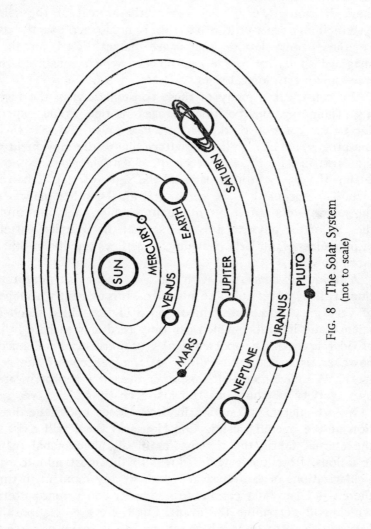

Fig. 8 The Solar System
(not to scale)

twelve sections which they named after certain constellations of stars which, in their time, were roughly in the centre of these divisions. (Today, because of the transit of the solar system in its great-year orbit, this is no longer exactly so.) To these constellations they gave names based on their imagined similarity to familiar objects, which constitute the well-known astrological signs.

We can observe many of these constellations in the night sky. Their apparent position changes, as one would expect, due to the rotation of the earth, but we also find that there is a progressive change in the pattern due to the movement of the earth in its orbit, as a result of which it appears to move during the year through each of the signs of the Zodiac in turn. This means that the earth, and all the other planets in the solar system, are in a continually changing relationship to the rest of the physical universe, so that the complex pattern of influences is similarly changing, sometimes rapidly, at others more slowly.

Astrology is concerned with the assessment and interpretation of this vast interplay of influences. It is evidently a subject of very great complexity involving a highly-skilled blend of science and intuition, which can only be discussed here in its broader aspects. The existence of extra-terrestrial influences, however, is a natural corollary of the concept of the real world. We have seen that this unmanifest realm is permeated by a variety of conscious transits, each of which gives rise to a particular manifestation in time. Hence under the direction of the overall Cosmic Consciousness there will exist in the eternal fabric the time-bodies of all phenomenal manifestations, from the galaxies down to the most minute particularizations of the physical world. At any moment in time there will be an intersection of these many concurrent patterns which will determine the event. But there are relationships between these patterns which extend in the realm of eternity far beyond the present moment, and these will be interpreted by the senses as rhythms.

Hence it is possible to understand in quite practical terms

how the earth and its inhabitants are constantly subject to celestial influences, even though we may only be aware of those which emanate from near-by bodies like the Sun and Moon. We have seen how these influences will vary as the earth moves in its orbit round the Sun, but there is a further much longer rhythm caused by the fact that the Sun itself, with its accompanying planetary system, is also moving through space. It appears to be travelling in an orbit round a star called Alcyone—the brightest star in a group called the Pleiades. The circuit takes some 25,800 years, which is called the Great Year, in the course of which the whole system passes in succession through the signs of the Zodiac.

As a result of this there is a slow change in the quality of the cosmic influences over the centuries, which means that the possibilities available and, more significantly, their interpretation, change their character as the Sun moves through the signs. The process is very gradual, for each sign occupies 2,160 years, but the present disturbed condition of the world is said to be due to an impending transition from the Piscean to the Aquarian age, as is discussed in Chapter 18.

* * *

The signs of the Zodiac are said to possess intrinsic qualities so that people born under a particular sign have certain essential traits. The Sun is in the sign of Aries from approximately March 22nd to April 21st, so that a person born between these dates is believed to have the characteristics of this sign, which are ardent and extrovert. As the year progresses the Sun enters each of the signs in turn, inducing corresponding characteristics in people born in the respective months.

However, this is a gross over-simplification. The Sun sign would seem to indicate the essential qualities of the person, in respect of their natural aptitude or inclinations, such as doctor, scientist, poet, farmer, etc. But the manner in which this is implemented is dependent on many other influences which operate through their lives from birth onwards. Astrologers ascribe particular tendencies to various planets. Thus Mars is associated with aggression, Jupiter with cheerfulness, and Saturn with limitation and restriction. Mercury was traditionally the messenger of the gods, and so is associated with mental activity, While Venus communicates harmony and unison. There is an elaborate technique for assessing the effect of these influences, which takes into account not only the planets involved but their aspects to one another. If they are occupying the same relative position in the heavens at the time they are said to be in conjunction, and their influence is strengthened. If they are in opposition the influence is weakened, or even inimical, while certain other angular relationships have corresponding interpretations. A valid horoscope must take into account all these influences as they relate to the specific individual.

Because the technique is almost entirely empirical it is viewed with suspicion by the logical mind. However, attempts have been made with some success to obtain scientific verification of astrological assessments. Vernon Clark, an American psychologist, collected horoscopes from ten people who had been occupied for some time in a variety of professions, namely a musician, a librarian, a veterinary surgeon, an art critic, a prostitute, a book-keeper, a herpetologist, an art teacher, a puppeteer and a pediatrician. The horoscopes were given to twenty astrologers, with a list of the several professions, and they were asked to match them up. Seventeen out of the twenty produced correct or near correct scores.[39]

Further tests produced similarly convincing results, confirming that astrology is a genuine art. Its methods may be empirical, though it seems likely that they originated from a superior level of knowledge, based on interpretations by the paranormal senses of the intersecting time-bodies in the unmanifest world. From this point of view there is no difficulty in understanding that the conditions obtaining at the time of birth can be scientifically assessed, and that the likely development of these trends can be updated from time to time, not as a forecast of the future, but as an intelligent appraisal of possibilities, which can be of practical value if correctly understood.

* * *

We live in a world of rhythms, many of which are normally unsuspected. In particular, it has been suggested that human activities are influenced by a series of *biorhythms*.[15] According to this idea the bodily functions are subject to cyclical variations, rising to a peak at certain periods followed by intervals of reduced efficiency. There are said to be three such rhythms concerned with physical, emotional and intellectual activity, which follow a 23, 28 and 33 day cycle respectively.

This is compatible with the idea that the human mind is a multiple structure containing separate divisions for the direction of specific functions, as suggested earlier. It may be that each of these responds to appropriate cosmic influences. Certainly the emotional cycle of 28 days appears to correspond with the lunar rhythm. The other periods presumably result from so-far unidentified planetary interactions. (One can detect a certain correlation with the orbital speeds of Mars, Earth and Venus, which are roughly in the ratio of 23, 28 and 33.)

It is claimed that these cycles start at birth and continue through the life so that by appropriate calculation one can estimate favourable periods for various kinds of activity, but this is a somewhat pedestrian interpretation of what may well be a much more significant potentiality. We have already spoken of the innate feelings of appropriateness which we frequently experience, but which are usually ignored in our preoccupation with the affairs of the moment. These may well arise from the vestigial sensitivity to planetary influences operating in the unmanifest realm, which can provide a measure of extra-sensory cognition.

The practical interpretation of planetary influences, in fact, is less concerned with the detailed assessment of their mechanism, but is better directed to the recognition of their existence as part of the essential harmony of the unmanifest pattern, to which the paranormal senses respond with a superior quality of understanding. From this aspect, a detailed (individual) horoscope can be of value, not in an attempt to forecast the future, but as an indication of the real pattern of the life, and the opportunities which exist for inner development. It is said that a conscious existence requires the full ultilization of the pattern of one's type, and that the fulfilment of human destiny involves a transit through the whole gamut of celestial influences.

CHAPTER TEN

The Dimensions of Eternity

In the early part of the nineteenth century there was much speculation as to the nature of life, which was generally believed to be associated with a property called animal magnetism. There was at that time little understanding of magnetism, and still less of electricity, both of which were interpreted with more imagination than science. Into this arena came a distinguished German chemist, Baron Karl von Reichenbach, who endeavoured to find a more rational approach to the problem. He came to the conclusion that life had little connection with the conventional ideas of magnetism, but was supported by a non-physical force which he called the *vis occulta*.

From this he developed, in 1861, the concept of what he called *odyle*, which was an intangible fluid permeating the whole of Nature, and which conducted the vital energy. He suggested that substances could be charged with this fluid, which could be transferred by contact; and that the human body was a container of odyle, which could sometimes be seen in luminous form as a coloured aura surrounding the body. Finally, he maintained that this fluid could give rise to an 'odic' force which could be transmitted over a distance.[38]

The idea was utterly rejected by his contemporaries who were reluctant to accept anything which could not be weighed and measured in physical terms. They were still finding it difficult to digest the concept advanced by Professor Thomas Young as early as 1804 that light was not a stream of luminous particles but was produced by wave motions in some all-pervading medium which he called the ether. This had been laughed to scorn in its day, but the researches of Fresnel, Faraday and Clerk Maxwell were providing increasing confirmation of its validity.

To accept the possibility of two intangible media was altogether too much, and von Reichenbach's ideas were ignored as mere speculation. Yet as is so often the case with ideas which are ahead of their time, they contained the germ of truth. Material science is concerned with the interchanges of energy involved in the physical processes of the phenomenal world. But within this realm there is the massive structure of organic life which is sustained by energy of a different quality, namely *vital* energy. We are normally only vaguely aware of this distinction because all living matter is sustained by the intake of physical energy in one form or another. Yet this energy supplied to a dead organism will not bring it to life, so that no amount of physical energy can create vital energy. The living organism, in fact, survives by virtue of an innate ability to transform physical energy into vital energy.

We will consider this process later, the significant point being that the phenomenal world is animated by the simultaneous operation of at least two distinct kinds of energy—an idea which contains exciting possibilities.

* * *

Let us look at some of the manifestations of physical energy which determine the appearance and behaviour of the world around us. Although it is an illusion of the senses, it is nevertheless a fascinating structure of transformations, mostly taken for granted. There are the changes of physical state, like the evaporation of liquids, or the variations of texture and colour resulting from chemical combinations of many kinds. There are frequent transformations of energy from one form to another. For example, if you strike a match, some of the chemical energy in the material is changed into radiation in the form of light and heat. All the time there is continual transformation of radiant energy into matter, as in the process of photosynthesis in plants. We should note, however, that all these are transformations—i.e. changes of form—of the same kind of energy, and do not involve any change of quality, for which a different kind of transformation is required.

All these aspects of physical behaviour are derived from the interchange of energy between and within the elementary atoms of which material is constituted. In the 1930's the atom was regarded as a relatively simple structure comprising a positively-charged nucleus around which negatively-charged electrons revolved like satellites. The concept, of which brief details are given in the Appendix, provided explanations of many observed phenomena, but closer investigation revealed subsidiary effects, to account for which it was suggested that the nucleus itself contained still more elementary particles. These cannot be observed directly, though they leave evidence of their presence in what is called a cloud chamber, which contains very finely divided droplets of moisture in which the sub-atomic particles leave a visible trail, rather like the condensation trails in the sky left by high-flying aircraft.

Pursuing this line of conjecture, nuclear physicists have postulated nearly one hundred sub-atomic particles, some of which have very odd properties. One, the neutrino, is virtually immaterial, having neither mass nor electrical charge. Others have an infinitessimally short life, and there are other peculiarities. It is unnecessary to discuss them in detail, because although there appears to be experimental evidence for their existence, science is beginning to suspect that this is illusory.

The mathematician Paul Dirac suggested in 1931 that space was not really empty, but was a fabric of ghost particles which were not detected by ordinary means. Occasionally one of these would be ejected from the fabric by a high-energy cosmic ray, so creating an observable particle—say an electon —and leaving behind a hole which would behave like an electron having the same mass but a positive instead of the usual negative charge, which he called an anti-electron or positron.

He suggested that this would have a very short life because the 'hole' would almost immediately attract a normal electron and the two would annihilate each other in a flash of high-energy rays. Although the idea sounded wildly improbable it received unexpected confirmation a year later from the observation of some electron trails in a cloud chamber which were deflected by a magnetic field in exactly the opposite direction to the normal. It was not long before more anti-particles were discovered, and it is now suggested that each of the fifty-odd hypothetical sub-atomic particles has its corresponding anti-particle.

The concept of anti-matter became widely discussed, though by no means fully accepted. There appeared to be evidence of these mirror-image entities, but no confirmation of the fabric of ghost particles from which they were deemed to arise. Richard Feynman, indeed, suggested in 1949 that an anti-particle was merely a normal particle moving backwards in time! All this speculation appears to be leading to ever-increasing complexity and is thereby inherently suspect. There is a well-known axiom called Occam's Razor, formulated by the fourteenth-century philosopher William of Occam, that the simpler the assumptions the greater the likelihood of truth. (His actual phrasing was 'the number of entities should not be unnecessarily increased').

Scientific thought is therefore tending to consider the possibility that all these hypothetical particles are merely illusory manifestations of relatively simple disturbances of an underlying pattern of force-fields pervading the whole phenomenal universe. There is even a tentative acceptance of the idea that this underlying pattern may be non-physical. The eminent astronomer V. A. Firsoff has related it to the idea of mind, as a universal entity out of which physical manifestations could be created through the operation of some transforming factor similar to Einstein's famous equation $e = mc^2$, which relates to the interchangeability of energy and matter.[12]

This equivalence is now taken for granted. Yet actually

THE DIMENSIONS OF ETERNITY

energy is *unmanifest*, being detected by the senses only as a result of its effects; so that there is in this interchange an implicit change of quality, which is not always recognized. By inference one can postulate that energy itself is a manifestation of some kind of activity within a pattern of force fields of a higher order beyond the evidence of the conventional senses. This would be the realm of unmanifest causes which has already been considered in broad outline.

* * *

Let us expand this concept slightly. We have seen that the unmanifest realm can be regarded as a kind of fabric of virtually unlimited possibilities. Within this territory influences travel which enliven some of the possibilities in their path, and thereby produce the manifestations in the phenomenal world which we call events.

We saw in Chapter 3 that this pattern could be represented by a simple analogy. The surface of this page can be considered as containing an infinite number of possible (unmanifest) points, a succession of which can be made visible by drawing a line with a pencil, as at AB in Fig. 9. This would

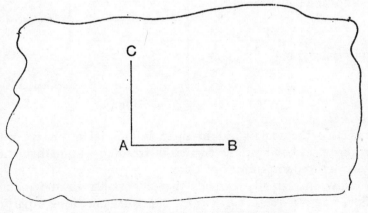

Fig. 9   Slice of Eternity

represent a movement of consciousness through the domain of Eternity. But it is clear that the pencil could equally well be moved in a direction at right angles to AB, as at AC, or in a variety of intermediate directions, any of which will 'actualize' a different selection of possibilities. So that at any moment the transit of consciousness has two degrees of freedom, which the physicists interpret as two dimensions of time—an idea postulated many years ago by Professor Eddington, and more recently by Adrian Dobbs.

Yet actually this is only part of the story, for the diagram of Fig. 9 only represents a kind of horizontal slice of the eternal pattern. Clearly there can be many such slices one on top of the other as illustrated in Fig. 10, so that if we are to

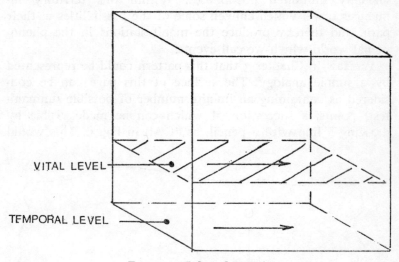

Fig. 10   Cube of Eternity

envisage the real world in these inferential terms we must regard it as having three degrees of freedom—in mathematical terms, three dimensions of time.

Now this greatly extends the potentiality of the pattern. For example, the consciousness which is generating a particular sequence of events in the phenomenal world could move to another level in the structure at which a different pattern of possibilities exists. This means that the interpretations provided by the conventional sense mechanisms can be substantially modified by a superior level of consciousness; and this will apply not merely to the human senses, but could modify the behaviour of any part of the natural world.

Moreover, within this more comprehensive structure, several conscious influences can operate simultaneously at different levels. Hence, concurrently with the ordinary transit of clock time, which will create the familiar experiences of the physical world, there can be other transits at a higher level which will create energies in the phenomenal world of a different order, which might not be detected by the ordinary senses. Such would be the case with vital energy, which can evidently accompany the manifestations of physical energy, but is of a superior, and incommensurable, quality because of the higher level of its origin, as is illustrated diagrammatically in Fig. 10.

The idea of different qualities of energy has many practical implications. The ordinary senses respond to the impact of physical energy—and we must remember that this includes the whole physical world, which we have seen to be a structure of response to stimulus. But they do not respond to the radiations of vital energy, of which we are normally aware only as a result of its effects on physical structure. It is only the paranormal senses which can respond directly to the impressions of vital energy, and these are very indifferently used.

Nor is vital energy necessarily the only non-physical energy in the phenomenal world. It is quite possible to envisage that other forms of energy exist beyond the detection of the physical senses, and these may well be the cause of various supernatural effects. Yet if so, it will be evident that no communication with these energies can be established through the physical senses, but only through the paranormal faculties, which can themselves operate at several levels.

* * *

It was this realm of vital energy which von Reichenbach attempted to investigate, and although his concept of odyle was inadequately formulated, he was entirely correct in his belief that life was supported by energy of a different quality from that of the physical world. Moreover, the existence of such energies can be understood without the need to postulate imaginary universal fluids, any more than it is necessary to assume the all-pervading ether of the nineteenth-century physicists.

This difference in quality was to be demonstrated in unexpectedly dramatic fashion by the work of a Viennese doctor, Wilhelm Reich, who attempted over a period of some twenty years from 1935 to 1955 to isolate vital energy. He believed that this was a universal property of Nature which he called orgone, and he endeavoured to concentrate this energy in devices which he called orgone accumulators. These consisted of boxes of sheet iron covered externally with organic material, the theory being that the organic matter attracted vital energy from the air which was transmitted to the inside of the box, but was then trapped by the iron inner coating.

The atmosphere inside the boxes certainly appeared to contain some therapeutic energy—some of the devices being large enough for a patient to sit inside—and he believed that he was obtaining some success in the treatment of cancer. This led him to a disastrous error. He argued that orgone energy might prove to be an antidote to radiation sickness, on the theory that inimical radiations arising from the breakdown of matter might be counteracted by the vital energy involved in its creation (without realizing that the two energies were of incompatible quality). He therefore placed some radio-active material in an orgone accumulator; but this produced an unexpectedly violent reaction which rapidly got out of control. Lethal radiations developed which not only produced extremely distressing symptoms in his co-workers, but began to spread outwards at an alarming rate, travelling at a speed of 30–50 miles a day. They were soon observed as far away as 600 miles, whereupon the American Authorities, in alarm, destroyed all his equipment, imprisoned Reich and his principal assistant, and burnt all his books.

The value of these ill-fated experiments, which are described by Dr Aubrey Westlake in his book *The Pattern of Health*,[87] would seem to lie in their confirmation of the essentially different quality of vital energy, so that any attempt to harness it in physical terms is potentially dangerous. It is clearly a natural energy of considerable magnitude—as it must be, since it animates the whole of organic life—and it must be treated with respect. Yet, rather than arrogantly attempting to control it, it is still possible, by the use of the paranormal faculties, to communicate with it and with this greater humility, successful contact has been proved to be possible, as is discussed in Chapter 12.

* * *

We referred earlier to the two aspects of transformation. One is concerned with changes of state within the same level of manifestation, as in the many physical changes in the familiar environment. The other involves a change in quality, which is a transformation to a higher, and incommensurable level. This is a significantly different operation. The Universe is not a static structure but is enlivened by the continual transfer of energy from one level to another, one of the examples of which is the transformation of physical energy into vital energy. The ability to achieve this is innate in all living matter, and is in fact its distinguishing characteristic.

This operation is, of necessity, directed by a higher level of intelligence. Consider briefly the transformations in the human body.[26] It receives food into the stomach where it is refined by the digestive processes into a condition capable of being absorbed into the blood stream. The process is reinforced by the intake of air and, not least in importance, the energies resulting from the multitudinous impressions which the senses receive from the environment. All this is controlled (unconsciously) by the intelligence of the instinctive mind, which directs that while the physical materials shall be used to nourish the cellular tissues, some part of the intake is transformed into energy of a superior quality—namely the vital energy by which the mind itself is sustained. The physiological processes are well understood and can even, with some difficulty, be duplicated in the laboratory, but not the transformation of physical to vital energy.

This is why attempts to explain life in physical terms are unsuccessful, for they do not take into account the essentially superior quality of energy required to direct the intricate and fascinating physiological processes. Moreover, there is a curious blindness in our interpretation of the mind. We accept as a matter of course that the physical body requires nourishment. It never occurs to us that the mind has a similar need.

Hence the cellular world of which living matter is composed is subject to two simultaneous levels of direction, one concerned with the development of its physical structure and the other with the creation of the transformations of energy which provide the nourishment for the directing intelligences.

If this second kind of nourishment is not adequately supplied, the organism does not flourish. With animals and plants the supply is maintained naturally, though it may be restricted by inimical conditions (in which circumstances it can often be augmented by human compassion).

Human beings in general, however, make poor use of their potentialities. Their activities are directed by low-grade energy, and even this is largely squandered in self-interest. One often speaks of being 'in low spirits', which simply means that the necessary transformations which re-inforce the vital energy are not being adequately performed. If one can discard some of the habitual anxieties and accept impressions of wonder and delight, the body is immediately invigorated.

We are well aware in practice of people whose presence leaves us drained of vitality. They are individuals who squander their vital energy in spurious activities such as self-pity or the feverish pursuit of material gain, and who seek to make up the loss (unconsciously) by stealing energy from those with whom they come into contact. These are the vampires of legend, who feed not on blood but on vital energy. On the other hand, there are people whose presence invigorates us. They have a harmonious relationship to the Universe which creates a surplus of vital and higher energies which they can communicate to others.

* * *

It is commonly accepted that energy and matter are interchangeable, in accordance with Einstein's classic equation. It begins to appear, however, that this must be integrated within the concept of an unmanifest realm of wider possibilities. We have seen that there are separate, and incommensurable, levels of energy in the structure, so that conventional interpretations are no more than a partial representation of the real situation.

There has been some move towards a greater understanding in the realm of nuclear physics wherein it is now suggested, as said earlier, that the constituent elements of physical matter may be continuously being created by forces operating within the ocean of anti-matter. Yet this is still only a partial formulation, for the unmanifest realm is of more comprehensive dimensions, and the production of physical energy-matters is only a part of its possibilities.

It is interesting to note that there has been a somewhat similar approach in the macroscopic world of astronomy, resulting from the discovery of so-called 'black holes' in the universe. Within the prodigious firmament tens of thousands of stars have been observed by astronomers and their characteristics have been estimated by various means. About one tenth appear to be very large, running at relatively low temperatures which gives them a reddish tinge, so that they are called 'red giants'; but the great majority, which are known as main sequence stars, have internal temperatures of the order of 5,000 degrees Centigrade similar to our Sun. They contain only the simplest elements, being in fact nuclear furnaces in which hydrogen is continually being transformed into helium with the emission of vast quantities of energy as is described in the Appendix.

There are, however, certain stars which are too small to dissipate this energy satisfactorily, in consequence of which their temperature increases, rising at the centre to 50,000 degrees or more. In these conditions the atoms in the core disintegrate into fragments and collapse under the weight of the rest of the star. Hence these 'white dwarfs', as they are called, are continually decreasing in size until ultimately the pressure becomes so great that they are crushed out of existence. This leaves what the astronomers call a black hole where the remains of a once giant star appear to have disappeared entirely out of the universe!

This is quite incredible by ordinary reckoning and to account for it Professor Wheeler of Princeton University has suggested that while the matter has ceased to exist in that part of space it has moved *into another universe*. This he calls Superspace, which he belives to exist eternally, being the fabric from which the existing (physical) universe has been created and to which it will ultimately return, to be replaced by another universe, not necessarily obeying the same laws.

Here again is the concept of continuous creation, though not in the simple terms postulated in Chapter 8. The tentative admission, in both macroscopic and microscopic realms, of the possibility of a region of unmanifest causes must be regarded as a significant advance. However, it seems that this realm is still envisaged in physical terms, whereas as we have seen it is of a superior, and incommensurable, quality, both in respect of its characteristics *and its directing intelligence*. No real understanding can be developed until this superior direction is acknowledged.

* * *

In one way it can be said that we already live in more than one world, for the paranormal senses respond to impressions of a different quality from those of the ordinary senses. It is possible here to indulge in a certain flight of fancy—which is admittedly pure speculation. We saw in Chapter 8 that McDonagh postulated that the process of continuous creation was achieved by a succession of pulsating rhythms. We also know that any sensory reaction is produced by a succession of stimuli, each of which has to be followed by a brief recovery time before the cells are ready to receive a further stimulus.

It is possible, therefore, to conceive that the various transits of consciousness through the field of Eternity are not continuous, but proceed in discrete steps, so producing in the phenomenal world a series of separate pulses with an interval between them, as illustrated in Fig. 11. However, the pulses

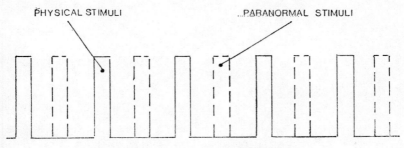

FIG. 11   Interleaved stimuli

produced by different transits need not necessarily occur together. There can be several such sequences of pulses timed to operate within the idle periods. This is, in fact, a recognized technique in modern communication systems, known as pulse-code modulation, in which a number of items of information are transmitted simultaneously over the same channel by a sequence of interleaved pulses.

Hence one can envisage one set of pulses which creates the manifestations of the physical world; but in between these there can be other pulses which can communicate information of a different order to which the physical senses do not respond, as indicated in the figure. These could create the manifestations of vital energy on which organic life depends, while still further pulses might be concerned with the transmissions of psychic and conscious energies.

It would be to these 'interleaved' pulses that the paranormal senses could respond, at their different levels. Nor need these necessarily be human. One can envisage that there can be manifestations at the physical level involving sense-mechanisms of a different character, so that there may be co-existing worlds obeying laws beyond the limited purview of the human senses, as was postulated by von Reichenbach.

This must be interpreted as no more than a glimpse of the truth. It is sufficient to recognize that a full development of the paranormal faculties would permit a response to a variety of influences beyond the range of the ordinary senses.

CHAPTER ELEVEN

Dowsing and Radiesthesia

Because extra-sensory cognition is essentially intuitive in character it may seem that its applications are largely of academic interest. However, this is not so, for there are certain directions in which the faculty can be put to very practical use. Under suitable conditions—of which the most important is a quiet mind—the paranormal senses can influence the muscular reactions of the body in such a manner as to indicate conditions or relationships which are not apparent to ordinary perception.

The most familiar example of such effects is the ancient art of water divining, which is traditionally performed with the aid of a forked hazel twig. The diviner holds the arms of the fork in his hands with the stem pointing away from him, and walks slowly over the territory to be examined with the idea of water in his mind. If there is a subterranean well or stream the stem of the twig moves sharply down (or up) as he passes over the spot. The art has been known from time immemorial and there are many references in the literature. Some early Egyptian bas-reliefs depict ritual figures holding a forked stick in front of them.

The use of the divining rod is not confined to the location of water. It was employed by fifteenth-century miners in the Harz mountains to prospect for minerals. From there it was brought to Cornwall by the merchant venturers in the reign of Elizabeth 1, where the art became known as *dowsing*, from an old word meaning 'to strike'. In recent times the technique has gained increasing acceptance and is used commercially for the location of subterranean materials of many kinds, including oil.

Nor is the traditional hazel twig essential, for equally positive indications can be obtained with equivalent forms of device, such as are illustrated in Fig. 12. Two strips of spring steel assembled in the form of a Y will serve equally well. Alternatively two rods may be used free to move in sockets

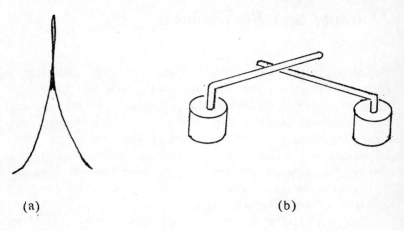

(a)   (b)

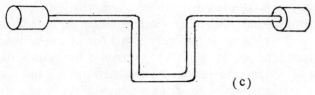

(c)

FIG. 12   Forms of divining rod

held in the hands, as at (b). These are normally held apart, but swing together when passing over the water or other substance being sought. A modification as at (c) is free to rotate about a horizontal axis, and it is claimed that the number of rotations gives an indication of the depth and/or size of underground deposits.

*   *   *

The consistently high rate of success obtained by experienced dowsers naturally attracted the attention of the scientific world. The first serious research appears to have been instigated in 1910 by Vicomte Henri de France, who was later associated with the formation in 1933 of the British Society of Dowsers. This resulted in a useful collation of experience, including an assessment of the qualities necessary in a successful dowser and the best ways of training people who exhibited some aptitude in the technique.

More recently official investigations, particularly in Russia, have confirmed the validity of the phenomena beyond question. Thousands of tests produced responses not only to subterranean water, but to minerals such as lead, zinc and gold at depths of over two hundred feet. Moreover, it was confirmed, as had long been known in practice, that the force on the end of the rod was quite considerable, being sometimes equivalent to a weight of over half a pound—technically a torque as high as 1,000 gram-cm.

Exhaustive experiments have been made to discover some physical mechanism for the phenomena, but without notable success. As with telepathy, there is evidence of minor physiological changes, but these would appear to be incidental. It has been observed, however, that dowsers are unusually sensitive to magnetic fields and can detect intensities of less than one per cent of the normal earth's field. Hence it has been suggested that hidden deposits of water or minerals can produce changes in the field pattern which the dowser can detect, possibly by some communication with the field of his own body.

There is evidence of the existence of 'dowsing zones' in which unusually strong responses are obtained, and there is some correlation between such zones and small changes in the magnetic field of the locality. However, this does not necessarily prove that magnetism is the cause of the effect. It may be merely a physical accompaniment to an influence of a paranormal quality, of which the possibility was discussed in the previous chapter.

The existence of such naturally-occurring fields is well established. Mice placed in an enclosure overlapping such a zone refuse to sleep therein but seek to get outside the field. Many plants, including hedges and trees, will not flourish if planted within a dowsing zone—which suggests a very practical application of dowsing. On the other hand it is said that ants and bees choose such areas for their nests.

There are many instances of locations which appear to exert harmful 'radiations' on the human body, of which the effect can be minimised by changing the position or orientation of a bed or chair, or by 'neutralizing' the influence by coils of copper wire. These are discussed more specifically in Chapter 14, the significant point being that the influence can be detected by the natural paranormal sensitivity, not by any means confined to human beings.

The most significant aspect of the faculty of dowsing, indeed, is that it can only be exercised through the intervention of a human interpreter. The influence, whatever it may be, will not affect a divining rod, or any of the other forms of detector to be discussed later, in isolation. Nor can results be obtained if the operator wears gloves. Personal contact is necessary, apparently directed by the operator's paranormal faculty.

* * *

The divining rod is by no means the only form of dowsing detector. It is convenient for prospecting, because it is not appreciably influenced by air currents or similar disturbances. An alternative form which is often used is a simple pendulum consisting of a small bob or weight on the end of a length of cord or chain.

There are two forms of this device. One uses a suspension several feet long, the actual length being adjusted according to the material being sought. If the correct 'tuning' is established, the pendulum begins to swing of its own accord and its behaviour provides the operator with the information required. The effect is attributed to some kind of resonance with the inherent radiations of the material in question. There is no physical evidence of the existence of such radiations but this does not preclude the possibility of rhythmic influences of a different quality, to which the paranormal senses respond. On the other hand, this apparent tuning may simply be an empirical method of establishing a selective rapport between the mind of the operator and the object of his search.

This is certainly the basis of operation with the alternative form of detector, the short pendulum illustrated in Fig. 13. This is only a few inches in length and is for many purposes the most convenient, being easily carried in the pocket. Its construction is unimportant for it has no intrinsic power, being merely an indicating device by which the experienced dowser can establish communication with the extra-sensory realm. However, this cannot be achieved by casual enquiry but only in response to specific and precise questions in the mind of the operator. Given this mental rapport the pendulum, if held lightly over the object or location under investi-

FIG. 13 Dowser's pendulum

gation, will react in various ways ranging from a simple oscillation to a gyratory motion, either clockwise or anticlockwise.

The meaning of this behaviour has to be interpreted by the operator from his own experience, for it may vary with different people, but having determined by experiment the significance of one's individual reactions the pendulum can provide answers to a wide variety of questions. It is essential, however, that these shall be clearly and specifically formulated in the mind of the dowser. For this purpose he will often touch with his free hand a sample or 'witness' related to the enquiry in order to strengthen the rapport. Some operators use a hollow bob in which is placed a sample of the substance being sought, but this may not be necessary if the dowser has a clear mental rapport with the subject of the enquiry, and has divorced from his mind any preconceived notions or expectations.

As a simple practical example, the Japanese use the technique to determine the sex of eggs in preference to the older practice of 'candling'. The eggs are placed on a conveyor belt with their long axes uniformly aligned on a north-south meridian and are interrogated by a dowser, whose pendulum gyrates clockwise for a cock, anticlockwise for a hen, but oscillates along the axis if the egg is sterile. It is claimed that there is a 99 per cent success rate.

The sex of human embryos can be determined in a similar manner, and there are many other ways in which dowsing is successfully employed. It can be used, for example, to assess the suitability of food or drugs. It will distinguish between natural and synthetic substances of (physically) identical composition. It can even determine incipient illnesses in a patient by dowsing a blood spot, as is discussed in the next chapter.

*   *   *

This kind of divining is sometimes called *radiesthesia*, which means sensitivity to radiations. One of the classic exponents of the art was Abbé Mermet, a French priest whose book *Principles and Practice of Radiesthesia*[18] summarized the results of forty years of experience and did much to establish a scientific approach to the phenomena. One may not entirely agree with his theories, but his practical achievements were astonishing. He was able to disclose the presence of water with incredible accuracy. In one instance (out of many) he predicted, from a map, that drilling 1·5 metres from a wall of a particular building to a depth of 12–15 metres would reveal a stream giving an output of 1,500 litres per minute. This was received with some scepticism, particularly since it seemed incredible that such a forecast could be made from a map, rather than on the actual site; but since all other methods had failed they made the drilling and found water exactly as predicted.

He had similar success with the discovery of oil and minerals, some on site, but many at a distance. On several occasions he located objects which had been lost, but his most spectacular successes were in the location of missing persons. On one occasion, a mother asked for information about her daughter of 15 who had been missing for some time. With a photograph of the girl as a witness and a map of the region he reported that it appeared she had fallen into a river nearby and that her body would be found at a certain place lodged in a bush; which proved to be the case. Another happier incident concerned a missing young man of 26. Having been given only the beret of the man as a clue the Abbé was able to trace him to Toulouse, 40 miles away, where he was found alive but suffering from a nervous breakdown.

These examples serve to illustrate the uncanny accuracy of divination which is possible. Although the Abbé Mermet was an unusually accomplished practitioner, similar performances are commonly achieved by experienced dowsers. The precise methods vary appreciably and it is unnecessary to dwell upon them in detail. The essential characteristic of the pendulum is that it is a responding mechanism, which will provide answers to intelligently and precisely-framed questions. To locate a missing object, for example, it is useless to ask vaguely 'where is it?' It is necessary to make an assessment of the possible areas in which it could have been lost, and to make an enquiry about each in turn. Having obtained a general answer, this can be followed by more specific questions, so progressively narrowing the search.

The same kind of approach is necessary in more sophisticated investigations. It is necessary to have an adequate awareness of the possibilities which exist. Otherwise it is impossible to formulate intelligent questions, and the response will be meaningless. Many of the failures or inconclusive answers obtained by beginners are due to vague questioning which amounts to no more than wishful thinking.

* * *

Why should the pendulum, or other divining mechanism, behave as it does? The material mind will seek to establish some physical basis, failing which it will decry the technique as a mere exercise of imagination or autosuggestion. Yet this is once again to confuse effect with cause, and any real appraisal must admit the influence of a superior level of intelligence.

As was said in Chapter 4, the essential characteristic of the paranormal faculties is that they *extend* the interpretations of the conventional senses. This means that the phenomenon of dowsing is brought about by the direction of physical behaviour by a superior level of understanding. To be unduly concerned with the mechanism only creates an unnecessary involvement in detail. One suggestion is that the paranormal senses produce involuntary muscular tensions which influence the behaviour of the pendulum. Alternatively, the response may be due to a modification of the body fields surrounding the fingers, which could produce psycho-kinetic effects such as are discussed in Chapter 16.

Whatever the mechanism, it is clear that the behaviour must not be adulterated by reactions dictated, even unconsciously, by the ordinary level of intelligence, which can only produce the answers one expects to obtain—maybe no response at all if this is what one expects! Considerable practice is necessary to achieve the necessary passivity of mind, free from the overwhelming associations of conventional activity. Given this detachment, however, the pendulum, or other device, can interpret *relationships* in the real world. This we have seen to be a fabric of interwoven patterns which the paranormal senses can assess beyond the limits of physical experience. In this realm the time-bodies of all objects and individuals are not transient but exist in an inter-connected and timeless relationship. It is only at the material level that these patterns are interpreted by the physical senses as independent objects and events, separated by space and time.

Thus each of the eggs on the Japanese conveyor belt has its own time-body which already contains its fulfilment. In cosmic time this will become manifest as a chicken, of already established sex (if it is to live at all); but whereas to the physical senses its development is not known until it is hatched, the paranormal senses are aware of the whole entity from its inception to its death.

The time-body of a mislaid object, or a missing person is similarly in existence *as a whole* in the eternal fabric, and the superior consciousness of the paranormal senses is aware of this entity, together with all its associated connections, which may not be apparent (or remembered) at the normal level of consciousness. All that is required is some physical or mental clue which will establish a rapport in the mind of the dowser and so provide a suitable starting point within the overall pattern.

In these terms the ability to dowse at a distance from a map is no longer utterly incomprehensible. The sample has its own time-body which is necessarily associated in the pattern of the real world with the location under investigation and can thereby provide the essential link in the mind of the dowser. I know in my own experience of the discovery of Roman remains of which the presence and location have been established from maps of the locality.

In like fashion a blood spot or sample of hair can be used to establish a connection with a person who is not actually present, and may be at the other side of the earth.

* * *

It may seem that although the possibilities of dowsing can be accepted, the faculty must be of limited availability. This again is not so, for Major General Scott-Elliot, the President of the British Society of Dowsers, has said that in his experience most people are able to dowse, only about ten per cent being insensitive. A further ten per cent possess unusual aptitude, while the remaining eighty per cent can become reasonable dowsers if they wish to, and can find a useful outlet for their ability.[30] This latter proviso is important, for the paranormal senses are of a superior quality and must be treated with respect. Magic is not for the asking but must be paid for, by dedication.

CHAPTER TWELVE

The Magic of the Body

Of all the familiar phenomena of daily life the one which is the most taken for granted is the body, with which we customarily identify ourselves completely. Because it is so intimately concerned with our activities we have a certain perfunctory interest in its behaviour. Yet its operations, and its possibilities, can be much better understood if it is recognized as no more than a mechanism, directed by a superior order of intelligence, which we inhabit for the purposes of existence on earth; and when this control is withdrawn, resulting in what is called death, the body has served its purpose and disintegrates into its constituent materials.

During its lifetime, however, the body is a mechanism of remarkable elegance and precision. Many of its operations are literally miraculous, though we take them as a matter of course. Its very structure contains clear evidence of a directing intelligence, as the eminent biologist, the late Sir Charles Sherrington, points out in his classic work *Man on his Nature*.[81] This is developed from a single fertilized cell, which divides into two; and these two again into 4, 8, 16, 32 and so on until after some 45 such mitoses there is an aggregate of more than 25 million million cells. But these are not all the same. At appropriate stages in the development some form themselves into bone, others into muscle. Some combine into elaborate assemblies of heart, liver, kidneys, etc., in readiness for the time when the embryo will emerge from the womb as an independent entity. Some form eyes which *later* will see; or lungs which *later* will breathe. As Sherrington says 'It is as if an immanent principle inspired each cell with the knowledge for the carrying out of a design'.

Yet this is only the beginning of the story, for after the body has been born it has to be sustained by a continuance of this direction. Not only have its many functions to be properly co-ordinated but there has to be the continual replenishment of the cells which die roughly once a day (though not all at once); and if the structure is damaged by accident or illness this operation is speeded up so that new tissue is grown. The body is not able to cope with a major catastrophe such as the loss of a limb, though in less highly specialized organisms even this is possible. For example, if a newt loses a leg or tail it will grow a new one. The human body, nevertheless, can carry out astonishing repairs by virtue of its innate intelligence, which physicians call the *vis medicatrix naturae*, or natural healing power.

All these operations, which are usually taken completely for granted, are directed by a co-ordinating intelligence which Gurdjieff called the Instinctive Centre.[21] This is a specialized sub-division of the comprehensive intelligence or mind which programmes the behaviour of the organism as a whole, in both its physical and psychological aspects. We have seen, however, that since the mind is of an extra-physical character it has to be sustained by energy of a superior order, namely the vital energy discussed in Chapter 10. This is basically of cosmic origin, but needs to be continually replenished by the transformation of the physical energies of food and other forms of nourishment, which is an inherent ability of living organisms. The body, in fact, is a remarkably organized refinery which should be acknowledged with respect and wonder.

It should be noted, incidentally, that vital energy is not exclusive to man. It serves to enliven the whole of Nature, so that human life only receives its appropriate quota. Moreover, this is not necessarily constant. In the spring of the year, as the plants and trees begin to awaken from their winter sleep, they make additional demands on the available supply so that human vitality is temporarily reduced, as is well known medically.

* * *

If the natural harmony of the organism is disturbed by accident or invasion by hostile influences, the Instinctive Centre creates additional programmes to deal with the emergency and draws on its reserves of vital energy. It often withdraws energy from other functions such as thought and feeling in order to conserve its resources. However, the derangement may be greater than the system can handle unaided, in which circumstances appropriate medical treatment may be provided. This is evidently necessary in cases of accidental fracture of a limb or damage to a vital organ, though even here the experienced surgeon is well aware of the body's natural recuperative powers which he respects and encourages by intensive after-care.

This may be reinforced in a variety of ways. One is to exercise influence at cellular level by supplying appropriate medicaments which can assist the relevant cells in their repair work. Medical science has discovered a great deal about the physiological mechanisms and has developed in recent years a wide range of highly-sophisticated drugs, many of which have produced spectacular results. These very successes, however, have created a tendency to over-ride, rather than assist, the body's own intelligence, sometimes with disastrous consequences. This is really very arrogant because the intelligence of the Instinctive Centre is of a higher order than the sense-based intellect.

Moreover, if the restorative process is made too easy, the proper functioning of the instinctive direction may be impaired, so that the enlightened physician makes only sparing use of these palliatives. Certainly the massive use of uneducated self-medication today, encouraged by commercial interests, is an unwarrantable interference with the natural healing power of the body, and is undermining the health of the community.

An interesting example of misguided interference was provided by a biologist who observed a crane fly emerging from its pupa case, and noted that it was having trouble in extricating one of its legs. He therefore helped it, with the best intentions, only to find later that this leg was permanently weak, not having been allowed to make the the necessary effort. A more tragic case was that of a small child who developed an inordinate craving for salt. His parents refused to permit this whereupon the child sickened and died, when it was discovered belatedly that it had been suffering from a rare disease for which the only remedy was a massive intake of salt.

The Instinctive Centre, in fact, is in constant communication with the cells of the body which have a complete awareness of their own specialist requirements, and Ouspensky once said that if we knew how to listen to them we could develop a new basis of diagnosis. Actually such communication is available through the paranormal senses. Animals know intuitively what is good for them, and if they fall ill their instinct guides them to the appropriate remedy. In man the faculty has been largely stifled by the conditions of civilization, though its existence is sometimes demonstrated dramatically.

There is the remarkable history of Edgar Cayce, a simple farmer's son who was smitten in his youth by a mysterious illness and fell into a coma. While his doctors were vainly trying to restore his consciousness he suddenly spoke in a clear voice, diagnosing his condition and specifying the necessary remedies, though in his normal life he had no medical knowledge whatsoever.[36] Subsequently he reluctantly agreed to try to develop this faculty for the benefit of friends or others with whom he felt some rapport. In the presence of doctors (and always without fee) he would go into a trance and prescribe remedies which were often unknown to orthodoxy yet proved astonishingly successful, and he continued to give consultations, with the approval of the American Medical Association, up to the time of his death in 1945.

He had neither recollection nor understanding of his prescriptions when he awoke, but he came to the conclusion that in his trance states he established communication with the (instinctive) mind of his patient, which knew at its higher level exactly what was required.

* * *

So far, we have considered the possibility of remedial action at cellular level, but the paranormal faculty possesses the much greater potentiality of communicating with the vital energy pattern which is the primary cause of the physical behaviour. The higher levels of the mind can not only reinforce the instinctive intelligence but can, if properly exercised, over-ride the existing programmes, which may have become distorted by inimical influences. These modified programmes can then provide changes in the cellular structure, producing a miraculous restoration of the essential harmony.

Ideally it should be possible to do this for oneself, but in practice the necessary detachment is lacking. The limited supply of vital energy is dissipated in anxiety and self-interest, though it is well known that if this useless emotional activity can be curtailed the whole organism is invigorated. More usually, however, the modification of the vital energy pattern has to be provided by an external agency, of which there are two main forms. One involves direct communication between the mind of the patient and that of the healer (or some natural reservoir of vital energy) which is known as faith healing or spiritual healing. Alternatively, use may be made of medicaments which themselves contain vital energy of the requisite quality.

Both techniques have been used in their appropriate context throughout the ages. Because they operate in the unmanifest realm they tend to be regarded with suspicion by orthodox thinking, which classifies them somewhat superciliously as Fringe Medicine.[11] Actually they should be regarded as complementary. There are situations where physical treatment is necessary, but this should be accompanied by the more intuitive understanding of the underlying pattern.

* * *

Spiritual healing is a very contentious subject, rejected by orthodoxy because it transcends 'natural' laws; but this depends upon the definition of natural, since at an extra-sensory level quite different laws apply. It is unintelligent to dismiss as superstition the possibility of a conscious modification of the vital energy pattern by the proper use of the paranormal senses. Such is the magic of the Kahunas mentioned in Chapter 4, or the miracles of Jesus of Nazareth. Moreover, there are many records of spiritual healing performed by ordinary people who can exercise these powers, without claiming to possess any exalted consciousness, but whose mind are not cluttered with the wasteful anxieties of conventional behaviour. Harry Edwards, the most famous of British spirit-healers, maintained that it was not mental concentration which was necessary to his operations, but mental *abandonment*.

Nor is a human agency necessarily essential, for there are locations which contain unusual concentrations of energy as is discussed in Chapter 14. These are the holy places of legend, such as the pool of Lourdes, which can produce miraculous restorations of the vital pattern. The influence may also be crystallized in individual relics or talismans of which the time-bodies, by reason of their association with saints or mystics, possess supernatural possibilities.

Orthodox medicine maintains that there have been no recorded cures which cannot be accounted for by natural causes. This is something of an over-statement, as for example the case of Jack Traynor recorded by Geoffrey Murray in *Frontiers of Healing*. The nerves of his right arm had been severed by machine-gun bullets, leaving it paralysed, while a head wound had damaged his brain and caused him to become epileptic. Orthodox treatment had entirely failed and he was regarded as permanently disabled. Yet after a visit to Lourdes his arm was completely restored and his brain repaired itself. This was technically the result of natural causes, in that the intelligence of the body had repaired the severed nerves and restored the functioning of the brain, but only as the result of a massive influx of vital energy quite beyond the contriving of the surgeons. The operation of the chain of authority just outlined must of necessity involve 'natural causes', because this is the way it works.

* * *

Let us look at the alternative method of reinforcing the vital energy by the use of medicaments which rely on their intrinsic energy content rather than their chemical constitution. Among these are herbal and flower remedies, which are often regarded as old-wives tales. Yet herbal medication was established in China long before Hippocrates, dating back as far as 3,000 B.C. The Roman historian Pliny mentions it at length in his Natural History, and believed that there was a herbal remedy for every ailment, if it could be found; and there is a standard English work on the subject published by Nicholas Culpepper in the middle of the seventeenth century.

By this time, however, the art had become associated with astrology in the belief that the potency of the herbs was derived from planetary influences, both intrinsically and in respect of the time of the month when they were picked. Because of this element of intuition the art made little real headway, although in the early years of the present century the pathologist Edward Bach endeavoured by the use of radiesthesia to place the art on a scientific basis; and his flower remedies are well known and used by many practitioners.

Meanwhile, however, another technique of energy therapy had been developing from the work of Samuel Hahnemann, a German doctor who, in the early part of the nineteenth century abandoned the brutal and inefficient methods in which he had been trained in order to seek a less violent approach. For this purpose he began to examine the ancient, but somewhat haphazard practice of homoeopathy, which is based on the principle that *similia similibus curentur*—like should be cured by like; so that an illness can be cured by the administration of a substance which in a healthy person produces similar symptoms. For example, belladona poisoning produces symptoms similar to those of scarlet fever, so that minute doses of belladona are prescribed as a cure for scarlet fever. However, this is a very superficial interpretation of the technique which is of a much more subtle character.[27]

With the assistance of a number of volunteers among his medical colleagues he established that the homoeopathic principle appeared to work, and accumulated a list of about one hundred remedies which he used with some success. The remedies were only used in very small, but rather arbitrary doses, and he began to seek a scientific basis to assess the magnitude of the appropriate dosage. It was here that, by accident of genius, he was to discover the real significance of the treatment. As a convenient way of measuring the dilution he adopted a method known as *potentizing* in which the dilution was achieved in a succession of stages. Thus a given quantity of substance was diluted with nine parts of inert material (e.g. water or sugar of milk) to provide a 10:1 dilution known as a 1x potency. One part of this was again diluted with nine parts of inert material to provide a 2x potency, and so on, until a 6x potency contains only one millionth part of the original substance.

Yet he found that it was still therapeutically effective, and that in many cases the efficacy appeared to increase with increasing dilution! He found moreover that this method of dilution had a special significance. For example, a 2× potency giving a 100 times dilution (10×10) was more effective than a simple 100:1 dilution in a single stage. So that, as is now recognized, the effectiveness of a remedy is dependent not only on the substance but also to a marked extent on the specific dilution or potency. Still more important, the correct potency is not determined by the disease, but by the *patient*.

Hahnemann concluded that the undoubted therapeutic effects of his remedies were not derived from their chemical constitution, but from some subtle energy content, which appeared to be preserved by the process of potentizing. Certainly a 6× potency would appear to contain an utterly negligible proportion of the original substance, and in many cases even higher dilutions are used. Yet it has since been established that such microdoses do have an influence on living tissue. For example, thyroxin in a dilution of only one part in five million has been found to influence the growth of tadpoles. Moreover, plants fed with homoeopathically-prepared nutrients show a markedly beneficial response.[9]

It seems that such medicaments are, in fact, operating at the level of vital energy, where they can influence the patterns in the real world which are the causes of the clinical symptoms. The practical difficulty is that the choice of remedy, and its potency, must rely to a considerable extent on the intuition of the practitioner. By experience an extensive *materia medica* has been built up, but since the very basis of the system is the treatment of the patient rather than the disease, it has remained a highly individual technique.

Recently, however, the development of the art of dowsing has provided a scientific method of assessing the relevant factors, but before discussing this we should refer briefly to Hahnemann's later concept of *miasms*. He had observed that whereas in many cases he was able to provide an amelioration of conditions which defied the orthodox techniques of his day, there were chronic illnesses which, though apparently successfully treated by homoeopathic remedies, continually recurred in modified form with increasingly distressing symptoms. This led him to look for what he called the 'primitive malady', and he formulated the idea that these recurring troubles were due to derangements in the vital energy pattern, which he called miasms.

The idea was rejected by the orthodoxy of his time, and even today is by no means fully acknowledged. Yet it is a concept which not only provides a basis of successful treatment of recalcitrant, and supposedly incurable diseases, but is consistent with the ideas of time-body discussed earlier. We saw in Chapter 5 that the events of life are the phenomenal manifestations of a succession of interwoven possibilities in the real world, and that these remain in existence in what is called the time-body. Now if an individual develops a serious illness this will be recorded in his time-body, and even though in the course of time the malady responds to treatment and is apparently cured, there remains a kind of scar in the time-body which may at some later time produce a further, apparently unconnected, illness.

This is Hahnemann's primitive malady, but with the facilities of his time he was unable to establish either its existence, or its treatment, on a scientific basis. It was not until a hundred years after his death that the development of medical dowsing made possible the systematic appraisal of the vital energy patterns.

* * *

The use of paranormal techniques in medicine really developed from an accidental observation by a San Francisco doctor, Albert Abrams, about 1910. He was percussing the abdomen of a patient suffering from cancer of the lip when he found a dull note in a certain area. He later found to his surprise that a similar reaction was obtained with a healthy patient who was holding in his hand a sample of cancerous tissue. From this he deduced that diseased tissue in general might radiate some distinctive emanation, and began to seek some form of instrument by which this might be detected.

He found that it was not necessary to use the patient as a 'sounding board' but that a hollow cylinder could be equally effective as a detector. A more significant discovery was that it was not even necessary for the patient to be present, since his condition appeared to be indicated quite satisfactorily by a sample of his blood, and by comparing this with the samples of diseased tissues he was able to diagnose the presence of disease. He also found that by varying the length of the wire between the blood spot and the detector he obtained a correlation with specific diseases.

This led to the development of the celebrated Abrams Box, which he offered to the medical profession as a new diagnostic instrument. The technique was investigated by other pioneers, notably Ruth Drown in America and George de la Warr in England. Unfortunately these 'boxes' were made available indiscriminately to people without adequate medical, or even

THE MAGIC OF THE BODY

scientific, training, which quite naturally aroused the antagonism of the orthodox profession; and although a committee of the British Medical Association headed by Sir Thomas Horder reported in 1924 that the system appeared to have some diagnostic validity, its practice remained highly suspect.

Nevertheless, the subject began to receive serious consideration by a number of eminent doctors, notably the late Guyon Richards, which was to lead to a new, and practical, understanding of the vital energies in the body. The pioneer of this work was a young surgeon, Dr George Laurence, F.R.C.S., who developed an inspired blend of the techniques of dowsing and homoeopathy which has become known as psionic medicine.[27]

Very briefly, the technique involves the interrogation of a blood spot, or other sample, by a pendulum in association with appropriate witnesses, from which it is possible to diagnose derangements of the vital energy pattern which may result from acquired toxins or inherited miasms. Reference is then made to selected samples of homoeopathic or herbal remedies which are known from experience to be appropriate, and the requisite remedy is indicated both in substance and in potency.

* * *

All these practices involve the exercise of the paranormal senses through which communication is established with the inherent intelligence of the body, and it is evident that this intuitive understanding is capable of practical and scientific development. It is unnecessary to postulate imaginary radiations. If the events in the physical world are seen as manifestations of the underlying patterns in the unmanifest realm one can comprehend that the paranormal senses will, *ipso facto*, be aware of the real relationships and possibilities which exist.

Within this pattern will be the time-body of a blood-spot or other sample, which by virtue of its connection in the real world with the time-body of its donor, can serve as a focal point for the mind of the dowser. This will be a continuing relationship, persisting through the subsequent life of the patient, so that there is no need for the practitioner to meet his patient, though the rapport is aided by a knowledge of his situation and history, and there are many records of the successful treatment of patients at the other ends of the earth.

CHAPTER THIRTEEN

The Assessment of Quality

It has been said by various philosophers that everything in the Universe is weighed and measured. Science interprets this in material terms as the law of conservation of energy, which means that in any physical or chemical reaction the form of the energy may be changed but the quantity remains the same. Yet there are other factors which are not so readily measurable, one of which is quality, for which we have no numerical standards.

How, for example, does one assess the quality of an old master? A detailed analysis of the constitution and texture of the pigments will tell us little, for its real character is determined by the expertise and emotional understanding of the artist. Today an entirely spurious assessment of such works is calculated in terms of human greed. Everything in modern society tends to be valued by what it will fetch in money, which is a very indifferent yardstick.

The quality of any manifestation is really determined by the influences with which it has been impregnated throughout its existence. So that a great work of art or music has a quality which is not derived merely from its physical form, but includes the inspiration of its creator and all the effort expended in its production. Irving Stone records, in *The Agony and the Ecstasy*, the trouble taken by Michelangelo to find a suitable block of marble for his Pieta, until he could discern the imprisoned beauty to be released by his craftsmanship. It is this unseen travail which gives the masterpiece its quality, subsequently enhanced by the emotional appreciation of generations of worshippers.

The lives of the great composers contain records of similar

emotional turmoil, both during and after the creation of their works, which become even more impregnated with the interpretations of their subsequent performances, and the emotional response of countless audiences.

It is evident that none of this quality can be weighed and measured in physical terms. It resides, in fact, in the time-body of the work, which exists in the pattern of Eternity. Hence the true appreciation of quality involves the use of the paranormal senses, which possess a wordless recognition of innate relationships. We have seen that some people display this sensitivity more than others, but actually the paranormal senses exist as of right, and one of the practical ways of developing the faculty lies in the recognition of quality, not merely in works of art but in the many ordinary experiences of life.

* * *

Swedenborg suggested that quality could be assessed in terms of relative usefulness, which affords a certain basis of comparison. A precision microscope is able to provide a wider range of information than a simple magnifying glass. A luxury motor car provides more comfort and facility than a purely functional runabout. But how does one compare either of these with a painting or the majesty of an Alpine scene? Both of these have aesthetic value which cannot be expressed in material terms.

One needs a wider frame of reference not restricted to material values. The Russian philosopher Gurdjieff maintained that the quality of any manifestation was defined by its place and potentiality in the structure of the Universe; but this structure must clearly include far more than the limited interpretations of the senses. We have already seen that there are different levels of intelligence operating within the phenomenal world, which is itself directed by the superior intelligence of the unmanifest realm. According to esoteric cosmology this is only a partial interpretation of a more comprehensive structure comprising a succession of world orders of decreasing in-

THE ASSESSMENT OF QUALITY

telligence and consciousness emanating from a Supreme Intelligence. This is enlivened by the passage of force down the system, through the successive stages of creation, accompanied by a return flow produced by transformations of energy at each level—a process which is called in Hindu philosophy the breath of Brahma.

Now without going into detail, which would be beyond our present scope, we can understand that within this concept of a living Universe the quality of any manifestation is determined by its relative ability to conduct the influences operating at its particular level in the structure. Gurdjieff expressed it succinctly by saying that the place of everything in the Universe was defined by what it eats and what it is eaten by, and in these terms he devised a numerical system of quality evaluation. For the present purpose this is only of academic interest, though it is described by Ouspensky in his book *In Search of the Miraculous*[21] which also discusses in detail the hierarchy of world orders.

* * *

In practical terms, it is evident that we live in a Universe of qualities rather than quantities, enlivened by continual processes of transformation. Even the realm of familiar experience is a fabric of largely unrecognized transformations, both in state and in level. The significant aspect of these transformations is that they are not gradual, but only take place when there has been an accumulation of a sufficient quantity of energy. Science affirms that energy exists only at discrete 'quantum' levels and that changes of state can only occur by a sudden jump from one level to another.

A simple example is the boiling of a kettle. The application of heat raises the temperature of the water, which expands in volume but is still liquid. The molecules gradually acquire more energy until at a certain level they suddenly change their state to a gas, i.e. steam, which has quite different properties and potentialities. However, this kind of transformation, which is only one of many, is a change of state within the same **level** of manifestation, namely physical energy. There are additional more subtle processes involving a change of quality, as in the transformation of physical energy into vital energy discussed in Chapter 10. Moreover, this is only one stage in the process, for there are still higher forms of energy which nourish in the deeper parts of the mind.[26]

Even in matters of everyday experience there are many aspects of quality which are normally ignored. For example, a simple piece of stone may have a variety of qualities. In its natural state its uses are limited. It may have a certain value as a habitat for simple forms of plant life, such as lichens. If it is hewn and dressed it acquires a superior value as building material, while if it is of the right constitution it can be worked on by a sculptor and will possess a still different quality as being able to convey impressions of beauty which are a valuable emotional food for man. Here are three distinct levels of quality which can be recognized if we think about it, but which are assessed without words by the paranormal senses.

Clearly there are different standards of quality, some of them of a very low order determined only by practical utility. My ordinary reactions, for example, have never discovered a use for the earwig which infests my flowers, but its purpose is well understood by the superior intelligence of organic life. This is a trivial example, but it is characteristic of the limited interpretations of conventional associations. The paranormal senses have an instant recognition, without words or judgment, of the place and purpose of many things which fall outside the ambit of our normal preoccupation.

* * *

There are other aspects of transformation which are of practical interest. One is that the process can operate in two ways, creating manifestations of either finer and coarser quality; both these occur simultaneously throughout the structure. The condensation of the material world out of the

THE ASSESSMENT OF QUALITY

unmanifest realm is an example of increasing density of manifestation; but the energies contained therein are continually being transformed into more refined form, as we have seen. In many natural processes the two operations are interlinked. For example, the digestion of food in the body is a process of refinement from coarser to finer quality, but the residues of the transformations, which are ejected as waste products, serve other parts of organic life. The carbon dioxide exhaled by the lungs is food for plants, as also at a lower level are the bodily excreta.

An interesting interpretation of this process in plants is given by Rudolf Hauschka in his book *The Nature of Substance* referred to earlier.[9] It is popularly supposed that plants derive their nourishment from the soil, but this is only partially correct. Plant substance in general is composed of compounds of carbon, hydrogen and oxygen called carbohydrates, and the process of growth can be regarded as starting in the leaves in which, by the process of photosynthesis, the energy of light is converted into a physical substance known as starch. From here develop two complementary processes. The influence of the Sun, first as warmth and later in more subtle form, initiates a sequence of ascending transformations. The starch is converted into sugar, which appears in the blossom, and then into still finer forms which appear as scents, oils and healing substances, and ultimately in non-material emanations which nourish higher levels in the Universe.

In contrast to this process of etherialization, as he calls it, there are processes of crystallization or condensation. The starch degenerates into a coarser carbohydrate called cellulose which forms the structure of the stalks and roots. These can extract essential water and other nutrients from the soil; and in certain kinds of (perennial) plant they also produce a condensation of the vital energy which is stored in the bulbs or corms in readiness for the next season. This is a very simplified exposition of the activity, which Hauschka discusses in detail; but he then goes on to develop a significant distinction between natural and artificial transformations.

Science has analysed the chemical constitution of the many natural products of plant life, including those small but vital constituents of nutrition called vitamins; and it has succeeded in creating synthetic compounds of identical constitution which are presumed to be equivalent to the natural products. Experience shows, however, that in many instances this is not true. For example, synthetic Vitamin C does not have the same beneficial effect as the naturally-occurring product in fruit. Hauschka maintains that this is because they are derived from a wrong place in the structure of the Universe and are therefore unable to conduct the right quality of energy.

The chemical distillation of cellulose produces a product known as tar. For a long time this was of limited use, but

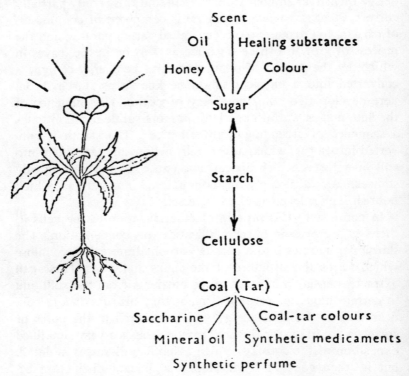

FIG. 14   Mirror-image structure suggested by Rudolf Hauschka

around the middle of the nineteenth century it was discovered that this substance could be broken down by the action of powerful acids which created a whole new range of compounds, notably the aniline dyes. This led to the foundation, largely due to the German chemist Friedrich Kekulé, of what is called structural chemistry, based on the discovery that carbon atoms can arrange themselves in hexagon rings, each corner of which has the possibility of combining with other elements or compounds. This opened the door to a bewildering variety of new synthetic substances such as dyes, aromatic oils, and medicinal preparations (e.g. aspirin) which are in common use today.

These Hauschka suggests are *mirror images* of the natural products and hence despite their apparent similarity are essentially different in quality. The idea is illustrated diagrammatically in Fig. 14, which is taken from his book, and shows the natural and artificial processes developing in opposite directions. In the plant the degeneration of starch into cellulose is the residue of a process of transformation directed by a higher level of intelligence. This is not so with the coal-tar derivatives, the production of which is directed by human intelligence, and thereby contains energy of a lower order.

* * *

It is this difference in the quality of the intrinsic energy which distinguishes natural products from the synthetic counterparts so much in use today. It accounts for the subtly different effects of the herbal and homoeopathic remedies discussed in the previous chapter. This is due primarily to the fact that they are prepared from natural substances which thereby contain the essential vital energy, and even allopathic remedies are more effective if they are derived from natural products. Moreover, there is a similar degradation today in the foods we eat, which are 'enriched' by an increasing variety of artificial substances.

It is not only in the medical and nutritional fields that our sense of quality is becoming degraded. We are living in an increasingly 'ersatz' world of synthetic materials which are cheaper or more convenient to produce than natural products. We use plastic utensils in preference to china or glass, without realizing that this is dead material containing the wrong quality of energy; but because there are no obvious ill effects we accept this as progress, and stifle the reactions of the paranormal senses which discern the difference of quality.

Our furniture is no longer made from whole wood, which contains an intrinsic life and experience in its time-body, and so has a quality to which the paranormal sensitivity can respond. Instead, we use fragmented materials like plywood or chipboard, or lifeless plastics, which are assembled in a purely functional manner and have nothing to communicate.

We have forgotten how to savour our food, which is assessed in terms of its calorie content, with no evaluation of its origin, or the care which has been expended in its preparation. Still less do we appreciate wine, which is regarded merely as something to drink instead of being savoured as a living entity impregnated with vital energy. This, of course, is not true of the connoisseur who is aware of the sympathy which a wine retains with its origin. It is known, for instance, that a vintage port goes temporarily sick when the sap is falling in its mother vine.

We are living, in fact, in an increasingly un-natural world, in which our precious paranormal faculties are slowly becoming atrophied.

CHAPTER FOURTEEN

Atmosphere

Most people are responsive, in varying degree, to what is popularly called the 'atmosphere' of a location. One experiences a certain feeling of exhilaration, or conversely an unreasoning revulsion, even amounting to dread. In occult jargon situations or objects are said to contain good or evil vibrations, though this is often derided as superstition. Actually, such feelings are derived from the exercise of an innate paranormal sensitivity which recognizes relationships of a different order from the interpretations of the conventional senses, and to dismiss them as imagination is just unintelligent.

These paranormal impressions are of two types, which can be loosely defined as temporal and spiritual. In the former category are the responses to a variety of influences which operate within the phenomenal world, but which are not readily explicable in physical terms. We referred in Chapter 11 to the existence of what are called dowsing zones, which are regions in which unusually strong responses are obtained with divining rods or other detecting devices. There appears to be some evidence of slight abnormalities in the earth's magnetic field in such locations, though it does not follow that this is necessarily the cause of the effects.

Whatever the reason, these locations are found to have a significant influence on organic life. It is well known that plants will flourish better in some situations than in others, although the physical conditions may appear to be identical. In particular it has been observed that if they are planted in a dowsing zone their growth is stunted, suggesting the presence of some inimical radiation.

It has been reported that mice will refuse to sleep in a

dowsing zone. On the other hand ants and bees are said to prefer such zones for their habitat so that the influences can be differently interpreted. Animals will exercise a peculiar preference for their resting place, often choosing a location which appears superficially to be much less convenient, while there are some places they will avoid altogether.

In human beings this sensitivity is largely stifled by the preoccupation with materialism, though it can be awakened as is described by a young American, Carlos Castaneda, in his book *The Teachings of Don Juan*,[5] which records his experiences with a Yaqui Indian in the Mexican desert. On one occasion he was told that there was a particular spot in front of the house which would convey a unique feeling of strength and happiness, but that he would have to find this for himself; this he ultimately achieved, resulting in a massive and almost terrifying influx of energy.

These influences, which appear to be very localized, can be regarded as resulting from some kind of radiation. Yet it is evident that this is not of a physical character, and from its influence on living matter one can suggest that it involves vibrations of vital energy which we have seen to be of a superior order. They will still be within the phenomenal realm, for vibrations (and energy) essentially contain the element of time, but they can only be detected by a different range of sensory equipment constituting the simpler levels of the paranormal senses.

We have hitherto made a broad distinction between the physical and paranormal senses, but it must be recognized that the paranormal senses themselves operate at different levels. They contain what can be called a mechanical part which operates at the level of the phenomenal realm, providing cognitive faculties which are not exclusively human but apply throughout the natural world. Moreover, they apply equally within the realm of so-called inanimate matter, for we have seen that this is continuously coming into being by the direction of the hierarchy of the creative minds.

* * *

ATMOSPHERE

One of the more subtle aspects of this sensitivity is the effect of physical shape. The more we discover about the structure of the Universe the more we find that it is essentially harmonious. Its many patterns are all developed from basically simple forms like the circle, or the sphere which combines maximum volume with minimum use of materials. Crystalline structures use equally simple symmetrical forms such as the hexagon and even the elaborate molecules of living matter are chains of basically simple units.

Man does not, in general, conform to this pattern in his artificial structures. He finds it more convenient to use rectangular or cubical shapes, and he designs these on a purely functional basis without respect to the cosmic harmony. Occasionally he chooses proportions which he feels intuitively to be aesthetically pleasing, but rarely with any real understanding. Yet experience shows that some buildings are more comfortable to live in than others. Some indeed have been found to act as reservoirs of vital energy, and to exert a curative influence on certain types of mental disorder.

If the relative proportions are arranged to be in tune with the universal harmony a structure can exhibit magical properties. This involves a certain translation from circular to linear mensuration which used to be called 'squaring the circle'. This is based on the ratio of the circumference of a circle to its diameter which is not a simple number but is approximately $22/7$, and is given the symbol π. Even this is not an exact ratio, being what is called a transcendental number, which can never be completely defined however many places of decimals are used. The usually accepted figure is $3 \cdot 14159$. (It may be noted that there are other transcendental factors in the physical world. Many natural processes develop at what is called an exponential rate, such that the growth or decay is always a specific proportion of the existing value, and this involves another transcendental factor e which is approximately $2 \cdot 7183$).

Now although every schoolboy is familiar with the use of the factor π in ordinary geometry—the circumference of a

THE AGE OF MIRACLES

circle, for example, is π times the diameter—the Egyptians discovered over 5,000 years ago that this factor had magical properties if it could be correctly incorporated into a structure. This they achieved in a variety of ways, the most familiar being the pyramids on the west bank of the Nile, which were built by the pharaohs as royal tombs around 3,000 B.C.

A pyramid is a structure comprising four triangular faces meeting at an apex, as shown in Fig. 15, but the significant feature of the Egyptian pyramids is that they were constructed

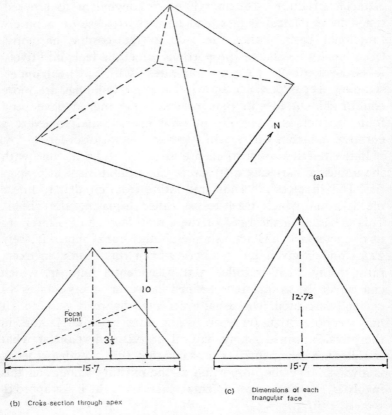

FIG. 15 Pyramid dimensions

to certain specific dimensions. If the four sides are each $5\pi = 15\cdot7$ units long and the height of the apex is 10 units, these proportions conform to the cosmic harmony and if the structure is aligned on the N-S meridian it exhibits magical properties. The influence is concentrated at a focal point in the centre of the pyramid one third of the way up from the base. It is not an arbitrary position but arises from the symmetry of the geometry which need not be elaborated here, and this is the location of the inner chambers in the Egyptian pyramids.

Various experimenters have constructed scale models of pyramids to investigate their supernatural possibilities. This may be done by preparing four triangles of suitable non-metallic material such as cardboard, wood or plastic to the dimensions shown in Fig. 15(c). Any convenient units may be used (e.g. centimetres) as long as the proportions are correct. The four triangles are then assembled as at (a) when they will be found to form a pyramid of the required height of 10 units, and an internal platform should then be provided $3\frac{1}{3}$ units up from the base.

A Frenchman named Bovis exploring the middle chamber of the Pyramid of Cheops observed the bodies of a number of animals who had strayed into the chamber and noted that despite the humidity they had not decomposed but had become mummified. He therefore made up a model pyramid to the required proportions and found that he obtained similar effects with dead animals placed therein, indicating that the normal processes of decay had in some way been halted. His experiments were later repeated by the Czech engineer Karel Drbal, who found further that blunt razor blades—at the time in short supply—became magically sharpened overnight if placed in his pyramid, though this is a rather trivial use of a property which has much greater potentialities.

There are, in fact, many more subtle possibilities which are only partially understood. Nor is the influence of cosmic harmony necessarily confined to pyramidal structures. It has long been known that in art forms there is a certain felicitous ratio of length to breadth which is called the *golden mean*. This has the peculiar value of 1·618 which appears quite arbitrary, but actually has a connection with pyramidal proportions. It will be noted that the triangles in Fig. 15(c) have a height of 12.72 units—not 10 as one might suppose. This is because they are mounted at an angle and the dimension is so chosen that when they are assembled they form a pyramid exactly 10 units high. Mathematically, this dimension is the third side of a right-angled triangle 10 units high and $\frac{1}{2}(15 \cdot 7) = 7 \cdot 85$ units wide. By the familiar Pythagoras relationship, the length of this side is $\sqrt{(10^2 + 7 \cdot 85^2)} = \sqrt{161 \cdot 8} = 12 \cdot 57$; and $161 \cdot 8/100$ is 1·618—the golden mean.

* * *

Why these cosmic proportions should create magical effects is not understood by conventional reasoning, which often endeavours to disprove their validity. The Canadian journal *New Horizons*, for example, organized a series of experiments with a variety of food stuffs which appeared to suggest that the onset of decay was not significantly influenced by the shape of the container; and one can discount any magical sharpening of razor blades by citing the well-known fact that a used blade will exhibit at least a partial recovery of its sharpness after a period of rest due to a natural release of internal tensions.

Yet it is easy to obtain negative evidence of this kind. Any purely materialistic approach is necessarily circumscribed by the quality of the questioning. No answers of a higher order can be expected unless the existence of higher levels of intelligence has been accepted in formulating the question. This is very clearly demonstrated in the art of dowsing, in which a rigid scepticism precludes any possibility of response.

We have seen that all the behaviour of the phenomenal world is directed by superior intelligence operating within the domain of Eternity. If the evidence of the conventional senses can be transcended, experiences of a different order become possible; but with a purely sensory and egotistic approach there is no communication with higher levels, and hence no magic.

The subtle harmonies enshrined in the Egyptian (and Mayan) pyramids has been the subject of intensive study ever since access to their inner chambers was achieved during the last century, and there is extensive literature on the subject which is quite beyond the present scope. There is reason to believe, however, that their particular structure contains records of akashic knowledge implanted by earlier intelligences, which can be interpreted in prophetical terms if properly understood.[3]

* * *

Let us now look at the second, and much more important aspect of extra-sensory cognition which arises from what we called spiritual impressions. It was said that the paranormal senses can operate at different levels. The lowest level responds to impressions which, while of a different quality from those to which the physical senses react, are still part of the phenomenal structure and hence contain the element of time. The higher levels communicate with the patterns of the timeless realm of Eternity and hence are able to assess the situation as a whole.

We have seen that we really live in two worlds simultaneously. The familiar world of appearances is brought into being by the successive interpretations by the ordinary senses of an already-existing pattern in the unmanifest realm. This underlying pattern is itself a complex structure of which the manifestation at any given moment in cosmic time involves the interplay of a large number of associated possibilities, and some of these may have far-reaching connections in the real world, so that at certain points there are concentrations of unusual potency. These are storehouses of the akashic influences mentioned in Chapter 3 and are manifest in the phenomenal world as the holy places of history or legend.

Such locations are impregnated with a higher quality of reality which is not measurable in physical terms. It is not really an energy, for energy is time-dependent and is continually dissipated. So that it is better to regard it as potentiality, derived from the pattern of a higher level. As a rough analogy one can liken the effect to that of a permanent magnet in which the molecules have been aligned by the application of a superior force, and thereafter continue to exert their influence indefinitely. The akashic force fields are of a different, but equally permanent quality, exerting influences to which the paranormal senses can respond.

These holy places are usually associated with the lives of saints or mystics, who have contributed their quota of effort and understanding, and have thereby left their footprints on the sands of time, as Longfellow expressed it; and the power is reinforced by the response of the many people who have refreshed themselves therein.

The influence is, nevertheless, mainly subjective, for if the paranormal senses are so overladen by materialism as to be virtually atrophied, there is little chance of response. I recall taking a visiting scientist to Canterbury Cathedral, but he experienced no sense of wonder, merely asking somewhat petulantly 'Does this mean anything to you?'. On the other hand, the willingness to listen which we call faith can permit a literally miraculous influx of vital energy, as with the pilgrims to Lourdes.

Sacred relics can also be impregnated with this superior potentiality, which can raise the level of experience, not by virtue of any mysterious 'vibrations' but because of the connections in their time-body with their origin and history. There is a similar power in some of the phrases of religious literature which not only reflect the being of their original formulation but have acquired a magical property from the devotions of countless generations—a magic which is greatly diminished by the current re-translations into popular language.

Even in everyday experience there are places or objects having a happy history which the paranormal senses recognize without words, while there are others with evil associations against which we react intuitively. Animals also exhibit this sensitivity, quite apart from the quasi-physical reactions mentioned earlier. But this is a very trivial exercise of senses which have much greater potentiality.

The characteristic of these reactions is that they are instant, and wordless, since they relate to a superior quality of experience. They convey the feeling of belonging to a Universe which *is*—which Zen Buddhism calls The-Totality-which-is-One,[13]—and they must not be degraded by attempting to analyse them.

CHAPTER FIFTEEN

The Plasma Body

We have seen that the world of appearances is only a partial representation of the real situation. This applies, in particular, to the physical body which is a similarly limited manifestation of a much larger entity beyond the evidence of the ordinary senses. The nature of this real structure must, of necessity, be largely conjectural but it can be envisaged as a pattern of potentialities which has a certain individuality within the unmanifest realm.

Within this pattern influences operate to generate energies of various kinds which permeate and enliven the physical body. Some of these create the familiar manifestations of the material world, but there are others, such as the vital and psychic energies mentioned earlier, which are of a different order not detected, as such, by the physical senses.

The body can thus be regarded as enclosed in a cocoon of interwoven energies emanating from the unmanifest pattern. This is sometimes called the 'plasma body'—a term which is used scientifically to denote matter in a pre-physical and dissociated state. From this arise condensations of energy of successively coarser quality.

The energies of a material order are detected by the conventional senses which relate us to the physical world and permit an understanding of its behaviour. The higher-order energies can only be directly apprehended by the paranormal senses, but it is part of their function to create physiological effects which can be observed in physical terms. However, if these are to be properly understood they must be recognized as secondary effects, subservient to causes of a higher order.

One of these effects is the presence of the weak electromagnetic fields which have been observed in the proximity of the human body—and of all living matter. These are physical manifestations of vital energy which the conventional senses do not detect, but which can be observed with sensitive equipment as was mentioned earlier. They produce what is called an 'aura', which is normally invisible but is recognized by the paranormal senses as part of the intuitive awareness which we call sensitivity.

Some people are able to observe these auras visually. They appear as a luminous fringe extending around the body for a distance of about six inches. They are of varying colour, depending upon the state of the individual, being brightest close to the body and diminishing in intensity farther away, often accompanied by streamers from the fingers or other protuberances. The haloes surrounding the heads of saints in mediaeval paintings are a representation of this field.

Not everyone sees these auras, but they can be observed under laboratory conditions. Walter Kilner, of St Thomas's Hospital, London, found many years ago that by looking through coloured glass screens he could detect a luminous shell round the body, and his experiments were later repeated by the Cambridge biologist Oscar Bagnall, who observed that while the aura was not disturbed by air currents, it was influenced by the proximity of a magnet.[2]

More recently, a remarkable technique has been developed by a Russian electrician Semyon Kirlian who discovered that by irradiating the subject with high-frequency electric fields, brilliant and scintillating auras became visible around any living substance.[20] They are vividly coloured and have been extensively photographed by Kirlian and others, notably Dr Thelma Moss of Los Angeles.

It is found that the colour and shape of the aura are dependent on the physical and emotional state of the person, or organism, concerned. In one instance a Moscow professor submitted two apparently identical leaves, picked at the same time. One exhibited a characteristic aura but the other showed groups of abnormal shadows, which continued to be evident despite repeated tests. When Kirlian rather disconsolately reported his results, the professor was delighted, for he said that the abnormal leaf had a malignant disease which was not visible to the naked eye.

Experiments with human subjects produced equally remarkable results. Not only were there marked differences in the auras of dead or dying tissues, but the physical or emotional state had a significant influence. In particular, the presence of pain induced patches of harsh colours, not normally present, which gradually faded as the pain was relieved.

It is found, in fact, that the aura of a person who is seriously ill is grossly distorted, but that it can be restored by the ministrations of a faith healer. During the treatment the fingers of the healer exhibit an intensely brilliant aura, clearly indicating the outflow of vital energy. Many years ago, before these visual techniques had been thought of, I witnessed a spiritual healer 'cleansing' the aura of a young boy who had contracted polio. He passed his hands repeatedly along the body, without actually touching it, pausing at intervals to shake off the filth. The proceedings were viewed with scepticism by the nursing staff, but in the event the boy made a complete recovery, against the medical prognosis.

Science is far from convinced by these experiments, seeking to explain them in terms of physiological changes, perhaps induced by the irradiation by which the auras are made visible. Yet even if such a correlation is established, it will only be an interpretation of the mechanism, and not the cause. The effects can be more significantly recognized as indications of the vital energy pattern which, as part of its normal functioning, can create manifestations accessible to ordinary sensory perception.

This can explain why people whose paranormal faculties are well developed can detect auras without elaborate scientific aids. Carlos Castaneda records that his Yaqui friend, Don Juan, liked to watch people, which he said are like luminous eggs if you really *see* them.[5] If he observed people without an aura he knew that they were not real—what Ouspensky called the 'walking dead'.

* * *

It is the understanding of this vital energy pattern which is the basis of the ancient Chinese art of acupuncture. According to their belief, the vital energy pattern is not static but circulates through the plasma body in a complex manner, and at certain points comes sufficiently close to the surface of the physical body to permit manipulation, either by contact with the finger tips of the doctor or by the insertion of small needles into the skin, so that if the pattern has become deranged an appropriate correction may be made.

There are some seven hundred such key points which, as a result of thousands of years experience, have been accurately charted. They do not correspond with any significant points in the physical structure, which is not surprising since they are concerned with the pattern of the non-physical vital energy. It is reported, however, that there is some correlation between the acupuncture points and certain bright-spots in the aura which appear under the Kirlian techniques.

The relevant key points have been comprehensively recorded, and prolonged study is clearly necessary to become familiar with them, but the successful practice of the art involves the use of the paranormal faculties which can assess the relationship in the unseen energy pattern. Given this understanding, however, quite remarkable results are achieved. Many common ailments can be cured, or better still prevented, by the restoration of the proper harmony in the vital energy flow; and this is effective with normally recalcitrant disturbances such as migraine.

Even more spectacular is the ability to produce local anaesthesia by inhibiting part of the energy flow. The Oxford don, Neville Maxwell, records having witnessed the removal of a tubercular lung under such conditions.[16] By the insertion of one thin steel needle in the patient's right forearm the whole chest area was numbed, permitting surgery to be performed with the patient fully conscious in other respects, and conversing with the theatre staff; and there are many other authenticated examples of such techniques.

As always, orthodox science endeavours to find physical explanations and to devise mathematical methods of locating and acting upon the relevant energy points. There persists this obstinate reluctance to admit the possibility of non-physical relationships which can only be properly interpreted by the paranormal senses.

CHAPTER SIXTEEN

Mind over Matter

The influence of paranormal intelligence is not limited to operations within the human body. The response of plants and animals to human intent has already been discussed, but the influence can be extended into the inanimate realm, sometimes deliberately but often unconsciously, producing effects which are known as psychokinesis, or PK for short, which means the control of physical movement by the mind.

It was, indeed, the claims of a young gambler to be able to influence the fall of dice at will which encouraged Dr Rhine to embark on his classic experiments on e.s.p.[29] He and his friends made 6,744 throws with a pair of dice, 'willing' them to fall such as to add up to more than seven. There are 36 ways in which two dice can fall, of which 15 give a total of eight or more, so that the chance of obtaining more than seven is 15/36, which would be 2,810 times out of 6,744. Actually they scored 3,110, a significant increase over chance expectation. Subsequent experiments showed that the success rate varied with the emotional state, and interest, of the operator, but a mental intention was essential. This was illustrated by the later development of a machine to make the throws. If each throw was initiated by an operator, 'willing' a certain outcome, the success rate after 170,000 throws showed odds of over 100 to 1 against chance, but when the machine was modified to make its throws at random, the results were no better than statistical expectation.

There are many other recorded instances of the exercise of mind over matter by individuals who appear to have some special ability in this respect. One of these was a middle-aged Russian housewife who was found to be able to influence the behaviour of an ordinary magnetic compass. By holding her hands six inches above it and willing it to move, the needle began after several minutes to change its orientation. She then started to move her hands in a circular motion, which the compass needle followed. Her body was reported to be under great tension during the process, but she was evidently creating a magnetic field several times stronger than the natural field of the earth.

This incident, however, remarkable though it is, is only one aspect of a wide variety of PK phenomena. It happens to be a phenomenon in which the mechanism is observable, though the cause remains a mystery. All that can really be deduced from the experiment is that the paranormal faculty can produce a modification of the natural body fields which can influence inanimate matter—in this case to a discernible extent. But there are other forms of control which are not so easily explained.

In recent years there have been a number of instances of miraculous modifications of natural behaviour which are so extraordinary as utterly to defy conventional standards. In 1963 an unemployed hotel porter, Ted Serios, often 'in liquor', was found to be able to produce images on photographic film by simply looking at a camera. This ability was extensively investigated by Jule Eisenbud, Professor of Psychology at the Denver Medical School, who established the undoubted validity of the phenomena.[7] In the presence of scores of reputable witnesses Serios has produced innumerable 'thought pictures' of buildings and objects, many of which he has never seen. In the main these were beyond his control, as if he were merely a passive observer of scenes floating through his subconscious awareness. Sometimes he could produce pictures to order, though in such cases they were often garbled or misinterpreted. For instance, when asked to produce a picture of the Arc de Triomphe he came up with an image of a Triumph motor car (in which he was far more interested).

The experiments were subject to the usual stringent controls to eliminate any possibility of deception, but the most baffling aspect of the performance was its apparent independence of external conditions. Wide variations of the local magnetic field had no effect; nor were the results affected if he was enclosed within a radiation shield having steel walls five inches thick. The thought pictures, in fact, appeared not to involve any known kind of radiation, the only abnormalities being the changes of heart rate, blood pressure, muscular tension and so forth commonly observed during paranormal states, which are secondary effects and not causes.

Some even more strange manifestations have been demonstrated by a young Israeli, Uri Geller, who is not only able to display conventional telepathic ability but can alter the physical structure or behaviour of objects by paranormal direction. He discovered this ability quite early in life—at the age of seven he found that he could cause the hands of a watch to move by willing them to do so—but neither he nor his family paid much attention because they regarded the effects as natural. However, when he was twenty three his powers came to the notice of the entertainment world, and thence to an astonished public.

During a B.B.C. television programme in the autumn of 1973 he followed some demonstrations of telepathy by causing a number of spoons and forks to bend, and even break, without the exercise of physical force but by merely stroking them and 'willing' them to change their shape. He also caused the watches of various members of the audience to stop.

There was a spate of derision from orthodox magicians who claimed that similar results could be produced by conventional illusions, though this could be discounted by the fact that a number of viewers found that similar effects had taken place in their homes during the programme. One might attribute this to auto-suggestion, but even so some supernatural agency would be involved; and several weeks later identical results were produced as a matter of idle curiosity by a young girl, Heidi Wilton, at her home in an Essex village.

Those who have met Uri Geller are impressed by his natural simplicity, and it is noteworthy that during his performances he does not exhibit signs of physical distress, which suggests the quiet mind postulated earlier in connection with telepathic activity. His abilities have been investigated under controlled conditions with complete success. He can reproduce simple line drawings in sealed envelopes and has read the face of a die enclosed in a steel box. He repeatedly causes the hands of watches to move and has repaired hundreds of broken watches without touching them. He even restored the functioning of a pocket calculator belonging to Wernher von Braun, the father of rocketry, by merely holding it in his hands. Actually this required two attempts. The first made it work, but in an un-co-ordinated manner, so he had to ask it again to behave properly. Finally, he has on occasion produced thought pictures on film similar to those of Ted Serios.

These and other phenomena are fully documented by Andrija Puharich in his book *Uri*.[24] As with all paranormal phenomena no rational explanations are forthcoming, and one has to regard the effects as resulting from communication with the underlying patterns in the unmanifest world.

* * *

These various manifestations are to some extent comprehensible as depending on the (possibly unconscious) exercise of human intelligence. In 1970, however, a Latvian psychologist, Konstantan Raudive, discovered some astonishing evidence of what appeared to be supernatural interference. In radio reception using a high degree of amplification there is a continuous background of noise resulting from small signals which are distributed at random over all the frequencies in the band. This is called 'white noise', (by analogy with white light which contains all the colours in the visible spectrum), and is used as a reference level in certain kinds of work. In the course of some investigations Raudive made a number of tape recordings of this white noise, and found to his surprise that when these were played back they contained fragments of mysterious voices.

This was naturally assumed to be the result of some accidental cross talk, perhaps from imperfect erasure of previous recordings or from interference from other equipment in the laboratory, but when the experiments were repeated under completely 'clean' conditions these mysterious voices were still present and even more noticeable. They appeared to be using a slightly different syntax from that of conventional speech, but were nevertheless intelligible, and over seventy thousand such tapes have since been obtained and analysed by voice-print machinery and other techniques, as he describes in his book *Breakthrough*.[25]

This would appear to be an entirely dissociated phenomenon which Raudive believes to be some kind of communication with past history, or possibly with other intelligences not of this world. At the same time, as the language began to be understood, it appeared that the voices would sometimes provide intelligible answers to question posed in the minds of the experimenters. There is here an evident correlation with the interrogation techniques employed in dowsing, as discussed in Chapter 11, so that the voices may not be as arbitrary as they at first appear, but may arise from the exercise of an unconscious paranormal intelligence.

However one interprets all these strange phenomena—and we shall suggest later a possible basis of understanding of the effects—the control of physical behaviour by paranormal direction must be regarded as established. Moreover, such control is not necessarily voluntary. There are records of miraculous escapes from disaster in conditions of emergency when the ordinary level of consciousness acknowledges its utter helplessness and throws itself on the mercy of the gods. Such was the experience of some war-time pilots who were saved from certain death by the power of prayer—which is a request to a higher order of intelligence, and can in emergency produce modification of physical conditions. These powers must not be invoked for trivialities, and certainly not as a kind of parlour trick. To attempt to utilize them for scientific investigation is perhaps permissible, though little success is likely if one seeks purely physical interpretations. The paranormal faculties are of great potentiality, which must be acknowledged with humility and respect. Gurdjieff used to say that to use them for frivolous purposes was like using a five-pound note to light a cigarette.

* * *

In addition to the effects so far described, however, there are instances of involuntary manifestations of PK, usually ascribed to poltergeists—a German word meaning a boisterous spirit. Pictures fall to the ground or clocks stop, often reputedly at the time of death of someone in the house. Objects are thrown about the room, apparently by supernatural agency, in a disturbing manner. It is now believed that these phenomena result from paranormal influences exerted, usually unconsciously, by some person in the house or locality.

An interesting example of this behaviour is recorded by Ostrander and Schroeder.[20] A young Russian girl, Nelya Mikhailova, was injured by artillery fire and spent a long period in hospital, during which time she began to develop strange powers. One day, when she was feeling very angry, she walked towards a cupboard, when a pitcher moved to the edge of its shelf and fell to the floor. Subsequently a whole gamut of poltergeist activities occurred, for which she began to realize that she was herself in some way responsible.

Her talents naturally attracted the attention of writers and scientists. On one occasion a visitor seeking an interview was startled to observe the cap of his pen being pursued across the table by a glass tumbler. Another writer who was dining with her observed a piece of bread moving across the table towards her and literally jumping into her mouth. It was evident that she possessed a marked sense of impishness.

Scientifically controlled experiments were instituted, with remarkable results. In one such test an egg was broken into a saline solution in an aquarium and she was asked, from a distance of six feet, to separate the white from the yolk, which she succeeded in doing after thirty minutes of concentration, during which very marked physiological changes were observed. Her pulse rate became irregular and very greatly increased, and there were endoctrinal disturbances characteristic of a state of alarm, while her brain pattern indicated intense emotional stress, with pronounced theta rhythms at a frequency of four cycles per second which appeared to be creating some disturbance of her body fields.

We referred earlier to the fact that the vital energy patterns appeared to generate magnetic and electric fields surrounding the body. On this occasion a newly-developed and highly sensitive instrument was used to record changes in these physical fields. It was found they exhibited marked pulsations during the experiment, which appeared to be triggered by the theta rhythms, becoming more pronounced and regular as the psychokinesis was achieved.

It has been suggested that these pulsating fields might be influencing the electron spin in the atoms of the materials being controlled, though just how is not clear. It may be that some such action is involved in all PK phenomena. However, as said earlier, any observed physiological effects must be interpreted as no more than the mechanism by which the requirements of a superior intelligence are implemented. The cause of the phenomena must be sought in the unmanifest realm.

One can nevertheless discern a significant connection between the theta rhythms and poltergeist phenomena. It was said in Chapter 5 that these rhythms are not normally present but develop under conditions of emotional stress. The mysterious and often violent misbehaviour of inanimate objects usually attributed to poltergeists may well be the unconscious result of frustration or emotional shock in some individual in the locality, particularly if they have an unusual paranormal sensitivity.

* * *

A further manifestation of the control of mind over matter is the phenomenon of levitation, in which objects are caused to rise from the ground and remain suspended in space for a brief, or even prolonged, period of time without apparent support. There are many authentic records of such effects, but because they can be fairly easily simulated by illusionists the idea of levitation is generally regarded with suspicion.

It clearly involves an abrogation of the laws of gravity, which we ordinarily regard as immutable. Yet gravitational forces are astonishingly weak by comparison with the electromagnetic forces within the atoms—actually 10^{36} times weaker. It is only because of the large masses of the earth and the heavenly bodies that gravity plays such an important role in our affairs. Hence the possibility of counteracting its effect is not difficult to contemplate, and is indeed contrived on a macroscopic scale in the now familiar conditions of space travel.

It is equally possible to envisage that this can be achieved at an atomic level by the direction of a superior intelligence. To some extent this happens naturally, for the intensity of the gravitational field varies with the locality and may even become reversed. A spectacular example of this is found in a small eminence near Moncton, New Brunswick in Canada, which is known as Magnetic Hill, where there is a weak antigravitational effect. Visitors are invited to stop their cars at the foot and release the brakes, when the car travels slowly uphill to the summit!

There are records of similar abnormalities in other parts of the world, but the art of levitation is more concerned with counteracting the force of gravity by conscious direction. For this there is considerable evidence both in legend and history. An account which is accepted as authentic relates to a mediaeval monk, Joseph of Cupertino, who was frequently observed during meditation to rise from the ground and remain suspended in the air. The public interest was so great that it disturbed the routine of the monastery and he was banished to his room where a private chapel was prepared for him.

In January 1874 Sir William Crookes reported in the *Quarterly Journal of Science* some astonishing demonstrations by the Scottish medium Daniel Dunglass Home, whom he had personally observed to rise from the floor on three separate occasions. At least one hundred such incidents were reported, and on one occasion, in the presence of three unimpeachable witnesses, Home floated out of a window into another room seven feet away, both windows being seventy feet from the ground.

The ranks of orthodoxy preferred to ignore such uncomfortable manifestations, but science today is prepared to investigate the possibility of forces which do not conform to established laws. Colin Brookes-Smith, for example, has shown that a heavy table can be induced to rise off the floor even though sensitive equipment fails to detect any conventional physical stimulus. At present only small-scale effects can be produced because any major manifestations can only be achieved by individuals who possess exceptional paranormal sensitivity, and these are very rare.

In the present climate of materialism, in fact, the art has been largely lost, but the possibility still remains. The *Puranas* of India speak of *laghiman*, defined as the power of making oneself light at will, and the Buddhist *Suttas* describe a similar power. Andrew Tomas, in his book *We are not the First*,[33] maintains that levitation was an accepted accomplishment in ancient times, and cites a number of instances of its use in handling heavy stones during the construction of religious edifices.

In a number of instances the exercise of levitation is accompanied by rhythmical chanting, which appears to induce a resonance with the cosmic harmony. We shall refer to this in the next Chapter, but it may be noted that many people believe that the massive blocks of the great pyramids of Egypt were set in position with such remarkable precision by the use of such methods.

CHAPTER SEVENTEEN

The Individual Mind

It is evident that no real understanding can be derived solely from the physical aspects of existence. Science is providing increasing reinforcement of our intuitive awareness of a different order of reality which is, by definition, of an extra-physical character. However, if this is to be more than an abstract idea we must examine more specifically the basis of our awareness.

Within the pattern of the real world the physical body must be recognized as no more than a temporary habitation for an immaterial entity of a higher order. This is customarily called the soul, though this should be regarded as a broad term for an unmanifest structure having several different levels and potentialities. The lowest of these levels, which Gurdjieff called Essence, is required to inhabit a physical body for the purpose of extracting a certain kind of nourishment from the experiences of the phenomenal world.[21]

In order to do this, Essence directs the behaviour of the body through an intermediate intelligence called the mind. This can operate at different levels, and should be subservient to the conscious control of Essence. In practice this is not so, for an interesting reason. When, at birth, Essence is first ensconced in its physical habitation its immediate concern must be to accommodate itself to the environment. To this end it instructs the mind to create tentative interpretations of the information supplied by the senses, which by experience gradually become co-ordinated into a consistent pattern.

However, these programmes quickly become stereotyped, so that the experiences of life no longer have the vivid quality which can enliven the deeper parts of the mind. What should be a merely preliminary exercise becomes accepted as the norm and the mind, in effect, goes to sleep, being entirely satisfied with mundane programmes which require a purely perfunctory attention.

What is not realized in this state of complacency is that virtually none of these programmes is our own. They have all been acquired, of necessity, from other people in the normal course of upbringing and education. They become modified by experience, which creates the illusion of independence, but this is only an extension of an already conditioned mind. Even the knowledge which we firmly believe to be our own is really almost entirely second-hand.

This means that in our day-to-day activities we do not exercise an individual mind. Our behaviour is dictated by ideas which have been implanted by someone else, largely in the past but quite often in the present. We are constantly swayed, unconsciously, by external influences which usurp the slender authority of the sleeping mind. This is very apparent in the devastating impact of mob oratory, or the pernicious propaganda of the mass media, but even in the trivia of daily existence our reactions are far less individual than is popularly supposed.

This is exemplified in the practice of hypnotism, an age-old art which was popularized in the early part of the nineteenth century by the Viennese physician Anton Mesmer. He found that by inducing in his patients a condition of artificial sleep he was able to implant suggestions to which they subsequently responded, without having any recollection of having been so instructed. The technique was neither understood nor accepted in his time—he attributed it to 'animal magnetism'—but mesmerism, as it was called, became a happy hunting ground for charlatans who played upon public credulity.

Today hypnosis is a recognized practice, though still imperfectly understood. By various methods, usually involving monotonous visual or aural impressions, the subject is lulled into a state of sleep, during which he can be given various instructions—for example, to perform some particular action at a given time or under specified circumstances. On being awakened he has no memory of these instructions, but will duly carry them out, apparently of his own volition.

This can be understood in terms of the mundane mind, which is lulled into a state of torpor. It surrenders what little authority it possesses and allows its functions to be usurped by the mind of the hypnotist, which can then formulate programmes to which the recipient will later respond unconsciously. It is evidently a situation which is open to abuse, though it appears that there are certain limitations. For instance, a person cannot be induced to perform what he believes to be a criminal act.

The medical profession makes a more legitimate use of the possibilities. A responsible practitioner can over-ride the established conditioning of a patient's mind with beneficial results, correcting confused and inimical relationships which have developed in the normal associative pattern. It is possible, moreover, to awaken the deeper parts of the patient's mind which communicate with his time-body, so that he can remember experiences in his past which are not accessible to normal memory.

The potentialities can even be implemented without the use of hypnosis, as such. It is well known that people can remember, or respond to, suggestions made during ordinary sleep when the brain is not so cluttered with trivial anxieties. It has been found that learning of new or difficult subjects can be aided by information provided by tape recordings played softly during sleep.

It is unnecessary to pursue these techniques in detail. It is sufficient to note that hypnosis is a specific example of the possession of the (sleeping) mind by an external authority. We regard this as exceptional, but actually it is so only in degree. In the customary state of psychological sleep the mind is frequently over-ruled by external personalities without our permission.

* * *

THE INDIVIDUAL MIND

We have the right to develop an individual mind which can operate with higher levels of intelligence beyond that required for the purely mechanical performances of life. However, these require energy of a different quality—the vital and psychic energies mentioned earlier which can only be produced by the transformation of experience.[26] In very early life, when everything is new and vivid and the sense of wonder is active, there is an abundant supply of this higher-quality energy; but we soon begin to take everything for granted, so that the mind is starved.

However, if this essential nourishment is maintained, the mind can exercise its true functions which are of vastly greater potentiality. It can operate at levels of intelligence comparable with those of the real world, with which it can thereby communicate. This faculty develops naturally in simple people who are not engulfed in the spurious anxieties of modern civilization, but for the most part they have to be cultivated by a re-awakening of the sense of wonder and thinking beyond the limited evidence of the conventional senses.

This individual mind can operate at increasingly intelligent levels. The first stage provides the simple paranormal sensitivity which recognizes the patterns in the unmanifest realm as a whole and so transcends the limitations of time and space which restrict conventional perception. It is the application of this sensitivity which permits the exercise of telepathy and clairvoyance.

This is a passive level which is vestigially operative to a much greater extent than is generally recognized, but is normally ignored. There are, however, levels of still higher intelligence which have the power actually to control physical manifestations. How this can be achieved is not so readily apparent but it can be understood in relation to the idea of continuous creation.

We saw in Chapter 8 that the perceptions of the ordinary senses create the illusion of a permanent environment whereas in reality all the objects of the physical world must be regarded as continuously 'coming into being'. The atoms and molecules of physical material have only a limited lifetime so that they are constantly dying and being replaced by fresh supplies. These are then incorporated into the structure in accordance with the pattern laid down by the appropriate directing intelligence, so that the various objects preserve their appointed character and appear to have a continuing existence.

This assembly programme, however, is not immutable. It is laid down by an appropriate part of the cosmic mind, but it can be modified at any time, either by accident or by the direction of a comparable intelligence. This can be exercised by the higher levels of the human mind which can thus produce miraculous changes of physical form or behaviour.

In these terms the many manifestations of mind over matter become at least partly comprehensible. One can envisage, for example, that the thought photography of Ted Serios is produced by a modification to the pattern of the photographic emulsion, in which certain molecules are re-created *as if* they had been exposed to light. In similar fashion, the structure of the spoons in the Uri Geller experiments is altered by a conscious modification of the normal assembly pattern which had been previously laid down during their manufacture.

The Raudive conversations are even more interesting for it seems that the molecular assemblies on the recording tapes are not being modified in an arbitrary manner, but have been influenced by interactions with the time-bodies of individuals who are no longer—or have yet to be—manifest at the phenomenal level in this part of passing time, but which nevertheless have a continuing existence in the pattern of Eternity.

The phenomena of levitation can be similarly interpreted, for we have seen that gravitational effects are inherently very weak and can be counteracted by relatively small changes in atomic structure directed by paranormal intelligences. In fact, an entirely new range of possibilities begins to emerge once it is recognized that the structures of the world of the senses are continuously being renewed subject to the direction of the laws of phenomenal cause and effect, but that this direction can be modified at any moment by the influence of a superior intelligence.

* * *

An important factor in paranormal control is the use of resonance. This is a familar technique in the physical world in both natural and contrived phenomena. By its use, influences which may be negligible in themselves can produce a significant result if they are timed to coincide with natural rhythms. There are many examples of this, one of the most spectacular being the shattering of a wine glass by sound waves. If such a glass is flicked lightly with the finger nail it will vibrate at its natural frequency and will emit a musical note. If a singer with sufficient voice control can produce, and sustain, a note of exactly the same pitch the wine glass will shatter. Random air waves will have an entirely negligible impact, but if they recur at exactly the right intervals the molecules in the glass will begin to vibrate in sympathy and the amplitude will gradually increase until the structure breaks.

A similar effect is involved in the control of mind over matter. The continuous replacements of the electrons, atoms and molecules have their own natural rhythms to which any modifying influence must be appropriately tuned if it is to be effective. The requirement is known to the higher levels of the mind without ponderous calculation, but in many instances it can be reinforced by the use of rhythmical chants or magical phrases. The classic example is the destruction of the walls of Jericho described in the Book of Joshua, but there are many other legends of the use of magical sounds in producing levitation and similar effects.

One can suppose that many of the physiological effects which are observed to accompany paranormal experiences are degraded manifestations of unsuspected rhythms of a higher order which are the real cause of the phenomena. The true exercise of supernatural power is a function of a quiet and patient individual mind. It is quiet in that its mundane activity is temporarily quiescent, and patient in the maintenance of the relevant rhythm sufficiently long for the necessary resonant build-up to occur.

* * *

The concept of the mind as an instrument of progressively higher levels of consciousness conveys a certain understanding of its potentialities, particularly in the possibility of exercising supernatural control by modifying the established orders of manifestation. Yet this over-riding direction clearly cannot be exercised indiscriminately, for this would lead to chaos. However, the quality of the superior levels of intelligence is such that they possess, *ipso facto*, an understanding of the real situation and are thereby subject to an appropriate restraint. Genuine magicians are well aware of what is permissible—which certainly does not include the abrogation of natural laws for personal gain.

Nevertheless such malpractice does exist, in the exercise of black magic, of which there are notorious examples. Yet one can understand that in the overall scheme there must exist the possibility of the misuse of natural powers, both in the realm of the occult and in the developments of science, as is only too evident today. One can postulate that some kind of balance is maintained by the direction of higher levels, similar to the balance of Nature mentioned earlier (page 69).

John Bunyan depicts the situation allegorically in the *Pilgrim's Progress*, where the Interpreter shows Christian a fire blazing against a wall with a man casting water thereon to quench it. Yet the fire burns higher and hotter, to Christian's amazement, until he is taken round the back where there is a second man with a vessel of oil 'which he did also continually cast, but secretly, into the fire'. (Everyman edition p. 36).

CHAPTER EIGHTEEN

The Aquarian Age

The most significant aspect of the supernatural phenomena discussed in the preceding chapters is that they are really quite normal manifestations of a superior level of intelligence, with which we have a right to communicate. Yet we have seen that this is not possible by the use of the ordinary senses, but only by the exercise of the latent paranormal faculties. This is not to decry the pursuit of knowledge, which is the most valuable attribute of the sensory level of intelligence, but which by its very nature can only provide a partial interpretation of the real situation.

There is today a bewildering proliferation of technical information which the ordinary individual finds increasingly indigestible, particularly as he is assailed by popular articles and television demonstrations which excite his curiosity but contribute little to his understanding. Hence we have not been concerned with elaboration of detail, but rather with the relationship of the phenomena to the superior levels of reality which science is beginning to recognize.

Now, this growing awareness of extra-sensory intelligence is no accident. It arises because the Earth, and humanity with it, is coming under new influences which create a different quality of understanding. We have seen that the phenomenal world is directed by intelligences of a superior order, and that these operations can be partially interpreted in terms of gradually changing celestial influences. This idea was discussed in Chapter 9, where it was shown that the annual orbit of the Earth round the Sun brings it into a continually changing relationship to the starry firmament. It is said, in fact, to pass through the twelve 'signs' of the Zodiac in succession, in the course of which there are small changes in the pattern of the planetary influences. These are normally unrecognized—apart from the farrago of nonsense in the popular press—but can be assessed in quite practical terms by people who have been appropriately instructed.

However, there is a much longer transit caused by the rotation of the Sun around the star Alcyone, as a result of which the whole solar system passes through the signs in the reverse direction to the yearly transit of the Earth. This is a kind of re-winding of the mainspring. It occupies 25,800 years of earth time, known as the Great Year, and produces a very gradual change in the quality of the celestial influences. In its transit through the Zodiac the solar system will dwell in each sign in turn for 2,160 years, during which period all its manifestations will be subject to the dominant influence of the particular sign, as illustrated in Fig. 16.

According to astrological lore, history involves a progression through a succession of ages, each of which sees the rise and fall of appropriate civilizations of significantly different character. It is claimed that within the limits of recorded history there have been six such ages, of which the general characteristics conform to the expectations of the dominant sign, in accordance with the pattern of cosmic evolution. At the beginning of each era there is a large influx of spiritual energy, but this is gradually dissipated, and the truths become distorted, so that a fresh injection is necessary.

In these terms, we are entering the Age of Aquarius, which is an era of spiritual enlightenment. The traditional representation of the sign is the Water Carrier—a man bearing a pitcher—and water in esoteric symbolism denotes truth. However, the characteristics of any age only develop gradually. The Piscean age from which we are emerging was characterized by a great expansion of knowledge, though during the first half of the period this was subject to the repressive influences of orthodoxy, so that for a long time the knowledge had to be kept secret. Once this barrier was surmounted, expansion was very rapid and is continuing into the present period.

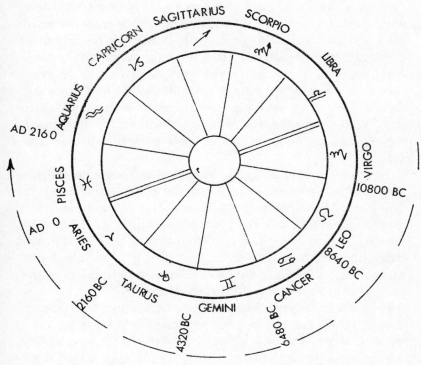

Fig. 16 Transit of Sun through the Zodiac

As a result, we are today suffering from an indigestible *quantity* of knowledge of purely material character. The Aquarian influences are creating a certain spiritual awakening whereby this knowledge can be transformed in quality, which is exemplified by the increasing discoveries in the realms of extra-sensory phenomena. It is said that as the new age develops these paranormal faculties will begin to be used as a matter of course, in place of the present exclusive reliance on 'facts'.

* * *

The impact of these new influences will be partly physical but mainly psychological, resulting in new interpretations of the experiences of life, and although we are not concerned here with spiritual development, we should examine briefly some of the implications. The influences will clearly not become fully effective for a considerable time since the Aquarian Age will last for 2,160 years, and in any case we have not yet completed the Piscean Age which has still another hundred years to run. Hence we are in a transition period in which there is a conflict between the waning influences of the preceding era and the more powerful fresh influences of the new age.

This is the situation foretold in Biblical and other prophecies; these prophecies were discussed by the late Maurice Nicoll in *The Mark*.[19] He cites the predictions by Christ recorded in the Gospels (Matthew 24, 3) of wars and rumours of wars, of famines, and pestilences, and earthquakes, which will characterize 'the consummation of the age'. This is often interpreted as signifying the end of the world, but it simply refers to the end of the *aeon*, and is really to be welcomed.

It would be irrelevant to attempt to discuss esoteric cosmology in detail. Yet it is possible to recognize in quite practical terms that we live in a Universe of far greater potentiality than is apparent to the senses. Moreover, it is clear that there are at the present time unusual opportunities to expand our awareness of the real situation.

We have seen that the body is no more than a mechanism through which to exercise the various physical and psychological activities which relate us to the haphazard experiences of life. Clearly, to derive one's meaning *solely* from expectation of the future is a very insecure and illusory exercise. The concept of a real entity which inhabits the physical structure creates a superior understanding which can *accompany* the necessary activities of the daily round.

At first this is no more than an idea which can account for many of the unusual phenomena in modern experience; but as one begins to stretch the mind in these directions, the ideas begin to infiltrate one's everyday reactions and create an enhanced awareness of the Universe as a whole. This is necessarily an emotional understanding, for reality cannot be expressed in words, but the paranormal faculties can provide partial interpretations which can shift the basis of one's interpretations.

One immediate consideration is that of mortality. If the physical body is merely a temporary habitation for an immaterial entity, this real body must have a continuing existence. This is an idea which is discussed at great length in esoteric literature, with varying interpretations which we need not pursue in detail. We can, however, consider the broad implications of the idea from a practical viewpoint.

We have seen that all phenomenal appearances are created by the transit of influences through a pattern of possibilities, not manifest to the ordinary senses, which we called the domain of Eternity. However, as was discussed in Chapter 10, this must be seen as a multi-dimensional pattern in which influences can operate at different levels. Hence one can envisage that the intelligence of the higher levels can create a variety of immaterial entities, conventionally termed 'souls', which are still part of the eternal pattern, but are of a lower order.

Now, within the structure of the living Universe these souls will be required to contribute a return of energy to their source, for which purpose they require a certain kind of nourishment. This is provided by the creation of the phenomenal world which supplies the material for a physical habitation in which the soul can reside. Through this mechanism it can then receive a variety of impressions which can be transformed into the superior qualities of vital (and other) energies which it requires for its development.

The phenomenal world, however, is governed by the laws of passing time, as a result of which the physical body only has a limited life. Hence the soul has to extract what nourishment it can during this limited period, and has then to inhabit a fresh body so that its development can proceed.

* * *

This is a very brief exposition of a concept which has many facets. The repeated habitation of a physical body is variously interpreted in different philosophies. It is necessarily a matter of conjecture, though the real situation is understood at the higher levels of consciousness. We can note, however, that since the soul resides in the unmanifest world it is not subject to the limitations of passing time. Hence it does not have to seek a 'future' body, but can inhabit any part of the cosmic pattern. This is an idea having wide-ranging implications beyond our present ambit, but it is of interest to examine some of the more relevant possibilities.

One very ancient idea is the theory of eternal recurrence which postulates that the soul continues to inhabit the same body repeatedly until it has acquired sufficient nourishment. This idea conveys a certain emotional understanding, for the essential nourishment can only be provided by transforming the experiences of life; and this requires the exercise of the metanoia spoken of earlier—the expansion of the mind which provides the interpretations of a superior quality to the stereotyped reactions of habit. Until this technique has been learned the soul is not adequately nourished, and is therefore starved.

An alternative concept, which is not incompatible with the idea of recurrence, is that of re-incarnation. Here the soul is deemed to inhabit bodies in different periods of cosmic time. Exponents of this idea cite many instances of individuals who claim to remember previous incarnations. Unfortunately many of these records are quoted in occult jargon, but within the scientific framework of the domain of Eternity the possibility appears entirely practical.

Nor is there any reason to suppose that these incarnations are necessarily sequential, or even isolated. In the pattern of the unmanifest realm, in which the soul resides, all places and times in the phenomenal world exist simultaneously, so that a given soul can occupy many parts of the temporal pattern concurrently; but one would expect that any 'recollection' of other incarnations would be interpreted in terms of time, because this is the language of memory.

One can thus envisage that a soul can inhabit many bodies at once. These need not be only in previous ages but can equally well be in the present, which could account for the rapport which exists between people, or groups of people. This idea is found in the Chinese doctrine called The Secret of the Golden Flower, which postulates that groups of individuals of similar spiritual stature are within the charge of a common guardian angel.

* * *

One of the disturbing features of the present era is the prodigious growth of world population. It is today a little over 3,000 million and is expected to double by the year 2000, which is causing ecologists some concern. The growth over the ages is a matter of conjecture since it is only comparatively recently that records exist, but it appears that human population expands in an exponential fashion, which means that the rate of growth depends on the value at the time, so that the larger the population the more rapidly does it increase. By applying this law retrospectively it is possible to estimate the possible population in earlier ages, one such calculation being shown in Table 2.

TABLE 2 *Tentative Estimate of World Population*

Date	Period	Population
AD 1970		3,000 million
AD 1550	Elizabethan age	400 million
AD 1	Birth of Christ	10 million
10,000 BC	Start of recorded history	1 million
50,000 BC	Neanderthal man	100,000
500,000 BC	Pithecanthropus	1,000
2 million BC	Paleolithic man	50

This is obviously speculative, but it is significant that the growth during the present era—the Age of Pisces now approaching its end—has been 300 times as great as that in the whole of the five preceding Ages illustrated in Fig. 16. This is a terrifying acceleration which suggests that humanity may be rushing headlong to its doom like the Gadarene swine.

There are some who believe that this is, in fact, happening but it seems more intelligent to recognize the existence of a cosmic plan of a higher order. The present conditions can then be seen as the implementation of an essentially simple pattern in the real world which, for reasons beyond our comprehension, is required to be manifest at the present time in terms of increasing multiplicity. This is certainly the characteristic of the present age, which may for that very reason provide greater opportunities for spiritual development.

* * *

In purely practical terms, the developments of the future—and the past—must not be assessed in terms of sense-based conjecture, which makes many unwarrantable assumptions, one of which is that the present civilization is the only one which has existed. There is ample evidence both in history and legend that the earth has not always been as we know it today. At certain periods there have been cataclysms which have devastated the established order, and destroyed the civilization of the time. The most well-known example is the legend of Atlantis, a continent believed to have been submerged beneath the ocean some 10,000 years ago, though this is now thought to be only the latest of a series of upheavals in the realms of pre-history.

Materialism regards legends with suspicion, but today a new climate of opinion is emerging which is prepared to accept them as genuine records of situations which have been directed by higher levels of intelligence, and in so doing has discovered geological confirmation of many of the ideas. There is a wealth of literature on the subject, to which we can here only make brief reference.

Immanuel Velikowsky has postulated in his book *Worlds in Collision*[35] that the solar system has encountered several vicissitudes. He suggests that at one time a giant comet crashed into the planet Mars, as a result of which the planet Venus came into being. This is an abnormal planet which rotates in the opposite direction to the others and has other peculiarities which have been confirmed by the space probe Mariner II.

This cataclysm disturbed the equilibrium of the earth giving rise to a variety of changes which are recorded in legend, including the displacement of its axis which caused 'the Sun to stand still' for a period, as recorded in the book of Joshua, and other histories. Even earlier legends suggest that at one time the earth rotated in a different direction, so that the Sun rose in the West.

Clearly the earth has had a chequered career. The Austrian engineer Hans Horbiger suggested in 1925 that it has had three moons prior to the present one, each of which in its turn was gradually overcome by the force of gravity so that it began to spiral inwards and finally crashed with devastating impact.[22] More recently, the American clairvoyant Edgar Cayce has said that there have been three such cataclysms, occurring roughly 10,000, 28,000 and 50,000 years ago.[6] Both suggest that in terms of cosmic time a further devastation is imminent.

There are clear indications that the present civilization is entirely transitory in cosmic time, and that there have been earlier eras possessing considerably greater expertise.[33] These have been discussed at length by Erich von Daniken in his book *Chariots of the Gods*.[36] He cites, in particular, the discovery in Turkey at the beginning of the eighteenth century of some ancient maps which proved surprisingly accurate in their central area around the Mediterranean, but showed a progressive distortion at greater distances. Yet this is exactly what happens with a photograph taken from a satellite, in which the outer regions are distorted by the curvature of the earth, and these maps have been found to correspond exactly with the terrain as seen from an American Air Force satellite located over Cairo.

In another place he refers to a 24-foot stone discovered at Tiahuanaco in South America which is inscribed with some remarkable astronomical data. However, these have been found not to correspond with present-day conditions, but to an earth having a year of only 288 days accompanied by a satellite making 425 revolutions a year. These are the conditions postulated by Horbiger at the time of the third moon period some 27,000 years ago.

There are many more such examples which von Daniken suggests are evidence left by earlier intelligences, possibly of extra-terrestrial origin, which become of significance to succeeding civilizations when their knowledge develops sufficiently.

* * *

What is the practical significance of these ideas at the present time? If they are interpreted as implying an impending breakdown of the existing civilization, this would seem to reinforce the current pragmatical attitude of 'eat, drink and be merry, for tomorrow we die'. Yet this is a sterile and irresponsible philosophy, for although it is entirely sensible to apply our hard-won knowledge to the increasing exploration of the physical world, it is ludicrous to suggest that the highest achievement of human intellect is the pursuit of comfort. Still less is there any validity in the arrogant assumption that man's destiny is to be the sole arbiter of the development of this planet, as has sometimes been stated.

History gives the lie to such conceit, for the pattern of events is controlled by intelligences of a higher order concerned with cosmic relationships of a more comprehensive quality not within the compass of the material mind. For example, medical research is rightly and responsibly concerned with the cure of disease and the relief of suffering. Yet its successes are continually offset by the appearance of new forms of derangement in order to maintain the cosmic requirement of limited mortality accompanied by a certain necessary quota of suffering.

In another field it is evident that the efforts of technology to ameliorate apparently unsatisfactory ecological conditions by the introduction of pesticides and artificial fertilizers, and the destruction of natural amenities in the pursuit of progress, are destroying the balance of Nature. But this is directed by the much more intelligent mind of organic life, which is introducing its own corrective measures. As Horace said in the well-known tag from his Epistles, written nearly 2,000 years ago, *Naturam furca expellas, tamen usque recurret*—though you drive out Nature with a pitchfork she will find her way back.

We are today much exercised by the squandering of our precious sources of energy due to the demands of civilization. As Dr E. F. Schumacher has pointed out, for every unit of energy which we extract from bread, over three units are involved in its manufacture, and a similarly uneconomic ratio applies throughout the mechanized processes of today, which are all directed to the minimization of human endeavour. Yet a subtle correction is already at work, derived not from human direction but resulting from the greed of the manipulators of the primary commodities, which may well lead, possibly painfully, to a return to simpler ways of life in the coming Aquarian Age.

One of the significant characteristics of the present transitional era is the increasing revelation of paranormal phenomena, from which is developing a scientific acknowledgement of the influence of superior orders of intelligence. As said earlier, the signs and portents which presage the end of an aeon do not necessarily imply physical catastrophies. There are relatively infrequent, but even when they do occur it appears that they do not take place without warning. They are developments within the pattern of Eternity of which the higher levels of human intelligence will have cognisance in advance, so that provision is made for suitable centres of consciousness which can preserve the truth as seed for the following era.

This is an idea which is contained in many legends, notably that of Noah's Ark which depicts allegorically the provision of a haven for real ideas in preparation for the impending destruction of the established order. The truth to be preserved, of course, is not material expertise, which indeed appears to have been greater in former civilizations, but is concerned with relationships in the noumenal world.

According to astrological lore this understanding will not be inspired in the Aquarian Age by a world Messiah, but will be fostered by small groups of individuals responding to higher levels of consciousness. This will be what Louis Pauwels has called the Age of Adepts, who will attract to themselves people who seek to transcend the limited interpretations of sense-based intellect.[22] It has been suggested that these Adepts may be re-incarnations of conscious men from Atlantean times who are living amongst us today for the preservation of real knowledge.

APPENDIX

The Chemical Octaves

One of the most elegant examples of intelligent design in the physical world is the pattern of the chemical elements. This has already been referred to briefly in Chapter 8, but it contains a number of intriguing potentialities which are worth closer inspection. It is found, for example, that the majority of the chemical atoms are deliberately incomplete structures and that the wealth of natural substances is produced by marriages between elements which are seeking completion.

This understanding, however, only developed gradually, beginning with the discovery by Dalton in 1803 that the various elements always appeared to combine with each other in definite proportions, which led him to put forward his theory of atoms. No particular pattern was evident because at that time only some 20 elements were known, mostly metals such as iron, copper, silver, gold and lead, together with carbon and sulphur, and the three most common gases, hydrogen, nitrogen and oxygen.

Certain distinctions had been observed, however, among the chemical compounds known at the time. In particular it was known that certain liquids, which were called acids, were of a corrosive nature, eating into metals with vigour and burning the skin. There were, however, other substances of a soapy character, like potash or caustic soda, which had a neutralizing effect, being able to combine with acids and render them harmless. They were given the name alkalis, from an Arabic word meaning ash. An everyday example of this action is the neutralizing of the effect of a bee sting, which is a mild acid, with washing soda.

APPENDIX

Dalton's work stimulated other chemists and in the next fifteen years nearly 20 more elements were discovered, and large numbers of hitherto unidentified compounds were able to be classified. Gradually it became evident that certain elements belonged, in some way, to the same family. Sodium and potassium (and later lithium) were all found to be strongly alkaline in character and formed similar compounds with simple acids. They are, in fact, known as the alkali metals.

A corresponding similarity was observed between the gases chlorine and bromine which are strongly acid in character. They form, with iodine, a group known as the halogens (salt-makers) because they all combine with the alkali metals to form salts of a somewhat similar character, found in sea water. In 1863 Newlands suggested that by arranging the elements in groups of seven, a series of chemical 'octaves' would result, similar to the musical octaves in which the various notes are repeated at a higher pitch in each successive octave. With this arrangement the similar elements each appeared at the same 'note' in their respective octave. The theory was received with some ridicule, but in 1869 the Russian scientist, Mendeléev suggested that if the elements were arranged in order of their atomic weight, they fell naturally into an octave structure such as Newlands had proposed, and he drew up what he called the Periodic Table of the Elements, which with certain modifications is still in use.

TABLE 3 *Simplified Periodic Table*

Group	Period 1	Period 2	Period 3	Period 4
I	Hydrogen	Lithium	Sodium	Potassium
II		Beryllium	Magnesium	Calcium
III		Boron	Aluminium	Gallium
IV		Carbon	Silicon	Germanium
V		Nitrogen	Phosphorus	Arsenic
VI		Oxygen	Sulphur	Selenium
VII		Fluorine	Chlorine	Bromine
VIII	Helium	Neon	Argon	Krypton

The discovery of the inert gases, neon, argon and krypton around the turn of the century seemed at first to invalidate the arrangement, but the difficulty was overcome by re-grouping

APPENDIX

the elements in periods of eight, and by placing the first two elements in a group by themselves as shown in Table 3, an apparently arbitrary arrangement which was to prove entirely compatible with the subsequent ideas of the nuclear atom.

The practical importance of this grouping is readily apparent. The alkali metals, lithium, sodium and potassium all appear in group I, while the halogens, fluorine, chlorine and bromine similarly appear together in group VII. Oxygen and sulphur, which are chemically similar in many respects, both fall into group VI, while carbon, which is the basis of organic life, is accompanied in group IV by silicon. The significance of this was not noted until much later, but today there is a whole range of artificially-contrived products known as silicones, in which the carbon atom is replaced by silicon, and which have remarkable properties.

All this, however, was an empirical pattern based on experimental observation. The underlying reason did not emerge until the discovery of the nuclear structure of the atoms themselves many years later.

* * *

Strangely enough it was the discovery that the Universe is based on *discontinuity* which led to the understanding of the real nature of the atom. For some time it had been suspected that it was electrical in character and, following Rutherford's discovery of the electron, various attempts had been made to picture the atom as a sort of miniature solar system, consisting of a central positively-charged nucleus with a number of negatively-charged electrons rotating around it; but these concepts failed to account satisfactorily for many aspects of behaviour.

In 1900, however, Max Planck made a discovery which completely changed the trend of scientific thought. This was that in any system, energy could only be absorbed or given out in definite (very small) amounts which he called quanta, rather like pouring peas out of a carton as distinct from a continuous flow like water out of a jug, and on this basis he formulated

APPENDIX

his now famous Quantum Theory. The magnitude of these energy jumps is very small so that the effect is not noticeable on a large scale but it becomes increasingly evident as we deal with smaller and smaller quantities.

Various scientists began to apply these ideas to the theories of atomic structure but it was not until 1909 that a young student at Manchester University, Niels Bohr, put forward the theory which appeared to explain all the observed phenomena, and is now accepted. He still assumed the atom to consist of a central positively-charged nucleus with a series of planetary electrons revolving around it in orbits, but he suggested that there was only a limited number of possible orbits, corresponding to specific quanta of energy.

If these possible energy levels are calculated it is found that nearest to the nucleus two orbits are possible. There is then a jump to a fresh level in which a total of eight orbits is possible. After this comes a further jump to a condition where a third series of eight orbits is possible, and so on. These different regions in which orbits are possible surround the nucleus like concentric spheres and are, in fact, known as the K, L, M etc. shells respectively.

The agreement between this pattern and that of the periodic table is immediately evident. The lightest of all elements is the gas hydrogen which has only one orbiting electron. This is followed by helium, also a gas, which contains two electrons, as shown in Fig. 17. These two occupy the innermost (K) shell which can only accommodate two orbits.

Then follow the eight elements in period 2 built up by the successive addition of electrons in the next (L) shell. Lithium has one, making three in all. Carbon has a total of six, two in the K shell and four in the L shell as illustrated in the figure. The final element in this period is neon with a total of ten electrons, two in the K shell and eight in the L shell, which is all that is allowed.

A further sequence then develops in period 3 with up to eight electrons in the M shell, a little farther out from the nucleus; and this is followed by the sequence of period 4.

APPENDIX

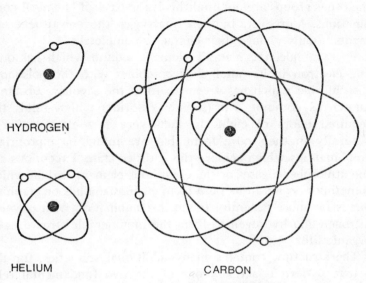

HYDROGEN

HELIUM   CARBON

Fig. 17   Simple electron orbits

Actually, there is a discontinuity in this period, for after the element calcium a subsidiary pattern develops which permits the addition of ten additional elements before the regular pattern is resumed, but we need not discuss this in detail save to note that the pattern becomes increasingly complex and ultimately becomes unstable which results in the spontaneous disintegration called radio-activity.

*   *   *

Now this pattern possesses a number of significant features, of which the most important is that the majority of the elements are incomplete, in that the electrons in their outermost shells fall short of the permitted number. The only exceptions are the elements in group VIII which do contain their full quota. These include the inert gases neon, argon and krypton, which are so called because they will not combine with any other element. They are, in fact, satisfied, whereas all those in

APPENDIX

the other groups are not, and this is the basis of chemical combinations. Moreover, in these marriages the constituent elements usually change their character completely.

For example, the metallic element sodium which has only one electron in its outer shell combines with the poisonous gas chlorine which has seven, to form the savoury substance known as common salt (sodium chloride) which fulfils the required quota of eight. In fact, very few elements exist naturally in their pure form, but are found in appropriate combinations which achieve this satisfied state. Exceptions are the atmospheric gases or the ubiquitous element carbon which sometimes occurs in its pure form, as in diamonds or graphite, but is far more generally found in combination with oxygen, nitrogen and hydrogen to form the innumerable structures of organic life.

The structure contains many additional subtleties, for the octave pattern is actually one of the two fundamental relationships in the Universe, which has wide-ranging implications. There is, for example, a certain discontinuity after the fifth note in the progression. Elements at this stage, e.g. nitrogen, have what is called a double valency, being able to combine readily with elements both earlier and later in the octave. The modern chemist is well aware of these subtleties and is able, by appropriate encouragement, to persuade atoms to group themselves into an astonishing variety of forms, with an expertise which evokes a profound respect. One feels that they themselves must often feel a corresponding respect for the underlying intelligence of the patterns which make their operations possible.

* * *

These relationships are scientifically established. However, if this octave pattern is related to the ideas of continuous creation discussed in Chapter 10 it is possible to regard the arrangement as a dynamic, rather than a static structure. The incorporation of an additional electron at each stage of the pattern necessarily adds its quota of energy, so that the sequence can be seen as involving a series of discrete increases in potential energy. In these terms, one can envisage that the intrinsic energy of the primary element, hydrogen, which is continually being replenished by its creation out of the unmanifest fabric of the Universe, overflows in a succession of discrete quanta to form the successive elements in the series.

The first stage is the formation of helium, after which the development occurs in a succession of octaves. The completion of each octave then represents a temporary resting state at which sufficient energy has to be accumulated to permit the initiation of a fresh octave.

This idea, of course, is no more than a broad appraisal of the possible pattern. The transition from one element to another involves more than the mere addition of an electron in the outer shell. Not only has there to be a corresponding additional 'proton' in the nucleus to maintain the electrical balance. The structure also requires the presence of certain extra particles called neutrons which carry no electrical charge, but merely add mass. This again is in accordance with a pattern remarkable ingenuity, which makes possible the release of vast quantities of energy locked up in the structure.

Nuclear physicists have discovered how to release some of this energy by the transmutation of one element into another, but the process operates on an enormously larger scale to provide the energy required for the maintenance of the whole physical universe. Our own solar system is sustained by energy radiated from the nuclear furnace called the Sun, by the continual transformation of hydrogen into helium. Two atoms of hydrogen, each containing one proton and one electron can marry to produce helium having two protons and two electrons. However the marriage requires the incorporation of two neutrons in the nucleus, which is not possible in ordinary conditions, but only at the temperature of some 5,000 degrees in the Sun's core, and when this transmutation is effected vast quantities of energy are released.

Here in practical terms is the beginning of the chemical series with the conversion of the primary element, hydrogen, into helium; and it is thought that at the still higher temperatures of some of the other stars in the galaxy this process may be extended to produce still further simple elements in the series. If this is related to the idea that atoms are continually dying—not all at once—as their intrinsic energy is dissipated, it is possible to envisage the continuous creation of the whole series, not merely in the stars but throughout the physical realm.

Such ideas, of course, are beyond the purview of orthodox acceptance, for which indeed they are unnecessary, because practical science is mainly concerned with the behaviour of atoms in the mass; and since these are continually being replenished there is always an adequate supply for practical purposes. But this need not preclude an awareness of the underlying intelligence by which these structures are directed, and the possibility of a progressive 'coming into being' as suggested in Chapter 8.

BIBLIOGRAPHY

1. Backster, C., Evidence of Primary Perception in Plant Life, *International Journal of Parapsychology*, 10:4, 1968
2. Bagnall, O., *The Origin and Properties of the Human Aura*, University Books, New York, 1970
3. Benavides, R., *Dramatic Prophesies of the Great Pyramid*, Neville Spearman, London, 1974
4. Brown, F. A., Persistent Activity Rhythms in the Oyster, *American Journal of Psychology*, 178:510, 1954
5. Castaneda, C., *The Teachings of Don Juan*, University of California Press, 1968
6. Cayce, E., *Atlantis*, Howard Baker, New York, 1970
7. Eisenbud, J., *The World of Ted Serios*, Jonathan Cape, London, 1968
8. Hardy, A., 'Biology and E.S.P.' (in *Science and E.S.P.*, Routledge & Kegan Paul, London, 1967)
9. Hauschka, R., *The Nature of Substance*, Vincent Stuart Publishers (now Watkins), London, 1966
10. Hixson, J., Twins Prove Electronic E.S.P., *New York Herald Tribune*, October 25, 1965
11. Inglis, B., *Fringe Medicine*, Faber & Faber, London, 1964
12. Koestler, A., *The Roots of Coincidence*, Hutchinson, London, 1972
13. Linssen, R., *Living Zen*, Allen & Unwin, London, 1954
14. Long, M. F., *The Secret Science at Work*, Huna Research Publications, 1953
15. Luce, G. G., *Body Time*, Paladin, London, 1973
16. Maxwell, N., *The Laughing Man with a Hole in his Chest*, London, *Sunday Times*, October 3, 1971
17. MacDonagh, J. R., *Protein—the Basis of Life*, Heinemann, London, 1966
18. Mermet, the Abbé, *Principles and Practice of Radiesthesia*, Vincent Stuart Publishers (now Watkins), London, 1959
19. Nicoll, Maurice, *The Mark*, Stuart and Watkins, London, 1954
20. Ostrander. S. and Schroeder, L., *Psychic Discoveries behind the Iron Curtain*, Englewood Cliffs, N.J., Prentice Hall, 1971

BIBLIOGRAPHY

21. Ouspensky, P. D., *In Search of the Miraculous*, Routledge & Kegan Paul, London, 1949
22. Pauwels, L. and Bergier, J., *The Morning of the Magicians*, Mayflower Press, London, 1964
23. Pengelley, E. T. and Asmundsen, S. J., 'Annual Biological Clocks,' *Scientific American*, 224:72, 1971
24. Puharich, A., *Uri*, W. H. Allen, London, 1974
25. Raudive, K., *Breakthrough*, Taplinger, New York, 1971
26. Reyner, J. H., *The Diary of a Modern Alchemist*, Neville Spearman, London, 1974
27. — *Psionic Medicine*, Routledge & Kegan Paul, London, 1974
28. Rhine, J. B., *Extrasensory Perception*, Bruce Humphries, Boston, 1934
29. — 'Dice thrown in Cup and Machine in PK Tests,' *Journal of Parapsychology*, 7:207, 1943
30. Scott-Elliott, Major-General J., 'Dowsing and its Applications to Medicine,' Hindhead, *Journal Psionic Medical Society*, Vol. 1, No. 6, 1972
31. Sherrington, Sir Charles, *Man on his Nature*, Pelican, London, 1955
32. Soal, S. G. and Bateman, F., *Modern Experiments in Telepathy*, Faber & Faber, London, 1954
33. Tomas, A., *We are not the First*, Souvenir Press, London, 1971
34. van der Post, L., *The Lost World of the Kalahari*, Hogarth Press, London
35. Velikowsky, I., *Worlds in Collision*, Gollancz, London, 1950
36. von Daniken, Erich, *Chariots of the Gods*, Souvenir Press, London, 1969
37. Walter, W. G., *The Living Brain*, Penguin, London, 1961
38. Watson, Lyall, *Supernature*, Hodder & Stoughton, London, 1973
39. West, J. A. and Toonder, J. G., *The Case for Astrology*, MacDonald, London, 1970
40. Westlake, A. T., *The Pattern of Health* (reprint), Routledge & Kegan Paul, London, 1973
41. Yakolev, B., *Telepathy Session Moscow-Novosibirsk*, Sputnik (Moscow), February 1968

INDEX

Abrams box, 134
Actualization of possibilities, 32, 53, 105
Acupuncture, 157
Adepts, 186
Aeon, end of, 178
Aka threads, 42
Akashic records, 31, 151
Alpha rhythm, 47
Amino acids, 56, 85
Amoeba, 63
Animal magnetism, 101, 169
Antimatter, 104, 111
Anxiety, 60
Aquarian age, 97, 175
Associative patterns, 18, 24, 56, 170
Astrology, 96
Atlantis, 182
Atmosphere, 40, 145
Atoms, 79, 187
Aura, 101, 155

Bach, Edward, 131
Backster, Cleve, 72
Balance of Nature, 69
Beta rhythm, 46
Biorhythms, 99
Bird flocks, 65
Black holes, 111
Blood spot, 134
Boehme, Jakob, 42
Bohr, Niels, 80, 190
Book of life, 57
Bose, Sir Jagadis Chunder, 72
Brahma, 139
Brain, 17, 27
— rhythms, 20, 44, 57
Buchan, John, 59
Bunyan, John, 174

Cage of time, 30
Casteneda, Carlos, 146

Cataclysms, 183
Carrington, Whately, 66
Cayce, Edgar, 128, 183
Celestial influences, 88, 176
Cellular level, 110, 127
Central nervous system, 18
Chemical series, 188
Circadian rhythm, 89
Civilizations, 183
Clairvoyance, 11, 58
Cognition, extra-sensory, 38, 45, 151
Collective unconscious, 41
Colour, sense of, 22
Coming into being, 29, 78, 171
Computer, 19
Condensation, 141
Conjunction, 98
Consciousness, 13, 35, 57, 67, 96
Consummation of the age, 178
Continuous creation, 84, 112, 171, 194
Cosmic harmony, 147
— intelligence, 66, 96
— mind, 70
— transit, 35
Cybernetics, 26

Dalton, John, 187
Daniken, Erich von, 183
Death, 125
Delta rhythm, 48
Dimensions, 106
Dirac, Paul, 103
Directing intelligence, 62, 92, 126
Discontinuity, 189
Discrimination, 27, 55
Divining (see (Dowsing)
Dog whistle, 22
Dowsing, 44, 86, 115, 133
— zones, 117, 145
Dreams, 60
Drosophila, 90
Drugs, limitations of, 127

INDEX

Eating, 76, 139
Education, of senses, 14, 42
Einstein, Albert, 37, 104
Electro-encephalogram, 46
Electromagnetic waves, 21, 81
Electron, 80, 103, 189
Elements, 79
Elementary particles, 80, 103, 187
Embryo, 125
Energy, different qualities of, 107
Essence, 168
E.S.P., 12, 45
Eternity, 33, 41, 58, 138
Ether, 101
Euglena, 89
Events, 33, 57
Evolution, 25, 70, 176
Exponential rate, 147, 181
Extra-sensory cognition, 11, 38, 45, 151

Fabric of Eternity, 32, 41, 58, 138
Findhorn experiment, 76
Force field, 152
Frequency, 20
Fringe medicine, 129

Gates, 55
Geller, Uri, 161
Genetic code, 56, 75
Golden mean, 150
Gravity, 90, 166
Great Year, 97, 176
Green fingers, 75
Group mind, 64, 92
Gurdjieff, G. I., 126, 138, 164, 168

Habit, 27, 56
Hahnemann, Samuel, 131
Haloes, 155
Harmony, 147
Hauschka, Rudolf, 83, 141
Herbal remedies, 91, 131, 143
Holy places, 130, 152
Home, Daniel Douglass, 165
Homoeopathy, 131, 143
Horbiger, Hans, 183
Horoscope, 98
Huna, 41
Hydra, 64
Hydrogen, 81
Hypnotism, 169

Illusion, 16, 78, 171
Immortality, 179
Impressions, 25, 34, 42, 151
Intellectual function, 27
Intelligence, 13, 27, 44, 74, 125, 184
Intuition, 40
Instinctive centre, 126
— functions, 27, 34, 128
Internal clocks, 92
Interpretation of information, 17, 60

Kalahari, 41
Kahunas, 42, 130
Kekulé, F., 143
Kirlian techniques, 155
Koestler, Arthur, 13

Laghiman, 167
Laws, orders of, 12, 49, 52, 179
Laurence, George, 135
Learning, 27, 42, 54
Levitation, 165
Lifetime (of elements), 84
Light waves, 22, 81
Location, extra-sensory, 121
Logic, limitations of, 27
Long body, 75
Long, M. F., 41
Lunar rhythms, 83, 90

Magic, 9, 42, 174
Magnetic field, 117, 145, 165
Map dowsing, 123
McDonagh, J. E. R., 85
Meaning, 25, 56
Memory, 54
Mermet, Abbé, 121
Mesmer, Anton, 169
Miasms, 133
Mind, 27, 35, 66, 159, 168
Miracle, definition of, 14
Mirror images, 143
Mitosis, 64, 125
Molecules, 79, 172
Mortality, 179

Neutrino, 103
Neutron, 193
Noah's Ark, 185
Noumenal world, 29
Nourishment, 64, 140, 171
Nucleus, 80, 103

198

INDEX

Occam's Razor, 104
Occult, definition of, 14
Octaves, 23, 187
Odyle, 101
Organic Life, 63, 88, 140, 185
Orgone, 108
Ouspensky, P. D., 14, 128, 139
Oysters, 91

Paranormal senses, 11, 38, 52, 122, 129, 146, 177
— direction, 163, 173
— impressions, 41, 151
Parapsychology, 12
Periodic Table of Elements, 188
Pendulum, 119
Phenomenal world, 29, 62
Photocell, 20
Photosynthesis, 63, 82, 141
Pi (*symbol*), 147
Pineal eye, 39
Piscean age, 97, 175
P-K phenomena, 44, 86, 159
Planetary system, 94
Plants, sensitivity of, 71
Plasma body, 154
Plato, 30, 33
Poltergeists, 164
Polygraph, 73
Population, growth of, 181
Positron, 103
Possibilities, actualization of, 32, 53, 105
Potentizing, 132
Prayer, 163
Pre-disposition, 56
Primitive malady, 134
Programming, 26, 63, 168
Protein, 85
Proton, 80, 193
Psionic medicine, 135
Pulsation, 85
Pyramids, 148

Quality, 137
— of questioning, 150
Quantum levels, 84, 139, 189

Radiations, 24, 70, 108, 146, 152
Radiesthesia, 120
Rapport, 51, 66, 75, 120
Raudive tapes, 162
Reaction time, 18

Recurrence and re-incarnation, 180
Reich, Wilhelm, 108
Reichenbach, Karl von, 101
Relationships, 59, 123
Replenishment, 84, 172, 193
Residues, 141
Resonance, 173
Response to stimulus, 18, 91
Retina, 20
Rhine, J. B., 11, 159
Rhythms, 20, 34, 90
Richards, Guyon, 135

Scent, 24
Schumacher, E. F., 185
Second sight, 38
Senses, mechanism of, 17, 63
Sensitivity, 40, 138, 146, 171
— of plants, 72
Serios, Ted, 160
Sherrington, Sir Charles, 64, 125
Sight, sense of, 20, 81
Sleep, 60, 89, 170
Solar system, 95
Soul, 168, 179
Sound waves, 22
Spiders, group mind of, 66
Spirit healing, 49, 85, 129, 156
Squaring the circle, 147
Stimulus, response to, 17, 63, 91
Structural chemistry, 143
Sub-nuclear particles, 103
Sub-sonic vibrations, 23
Supersonic waves, 23
Superspace, 112
Swedenborg, Emmanuel, 57, 138
Synchronization, 92
Synthetic products, 142

Telepathy, 45, 171
Theta rhythm, 48, 165
Third eye, 39
Thought photographs, 160, 172
Tides, 90
Timaeus Myth, 33
Time body, 57, 123, 138, 144
— lag, 18, 50
— scale, 53, 94
— sense, 30
Trance, 49, 128
Transformation, 79, 102, 109, 139
Transit, of consciousness, 35, 107
— of planets, 94

INDEX

Transit of the Sun, 97, 176
Translation of impressions, 24
Tuning, 118, 173

Understanding, 17, 43, 112, 168
Unmanifest realm, 15, 31, 52, 81, 105

Vampires, 111
Velikowsky, Immanuel, 182
Vibrations, 20, 146, 152
Vis Medicatrix Naturae, 126
—Occulta, 101
Vital energy, 85, 102, 133, 156, 165, 171

Vitamins, 142
Volvox, 89

Watson, Lyall, 90
Westlake, A. T., 42, 109
White noise, 162
Witness, 120
Wonder, sense of, 10
World line, 35

X rays, 22

Zen, 153
Zener cards, 12
Zodiac, 88, 94, 176